HOW TO
EXHIBIT AT
TRADE FAIRS

HOW TO
EXHIBIT AT TRADE FAIRS

The complete guide to making your company's next exhibition enormously rewarding

J O H N   A P P L E Y A R D

howtobooks

Published by How to Books Ltd
3 Newtec Place, Magdalen Road
Oxford, OX4 1RE, United Kingdom
Tel: (01865) 793806. Fax: (01865) 248780
email: info@howtobooks.co.uk
www.howtobooks.co.uk

British Library Cataloguing in Publication Data
A catalogue record for this book is available from the British Library

Produced for How To Books by Deer Park Productions, Tavistock
Typeset by Pantek Arts Ltd, Maidstone, Kent
Printed and bound by Bell & Bain Ltd, Glasgow

NOTE: The material contained in this book is set out in good
faith for general guidance and no liability can be accepted for
loss or expense incurred as a result of relying in particular
circumstances on statements made in this book. Laws and
regulations may be complex and liable to change, and readers
should check the current position with the relevant
authorities before making personal arrangements.

Contents

Acknowledgements

There are many people who have helped in the writing of this book and I would like to thank them all. I would like to mention Bill Richards of the Exhibition Venues Association who kindly allowed me to use statistics from UK Exhibition Facts.

Perhaps the greatest help was from Matthew Green, of Project Profile, who carefully read and advised on the original manuscript.

Preface

A couple of years ago, while we were working on some display panels for a large government department, a good friend and client bemoaned the lack of knowledge and experience among civil servants responsible for organising exhibition stands. Intense frustration was setting in when the job we were working on had reached its fifth or sixth version and still was not approved despite a looming shipping deadline.

'It's not entirely their fault,' my friend sighed. 'They get shunted into doing exhibitions from all sorts of other jobs in the department. Then they're given an enormous budget and told to get on with it. They really have no idea what they are doing. There ought to be a simple book I could give them to help, but I just can't find one anywhere.'

I didn't believe him. Then I looked around libraries and bookshops. The only books I could find were some from the States, where attitudes to exhibitions are somewhat different from those in Europe. The following pages were written to fill that gap. I hope they help you. If you feel I have missed anything, I apologise. Contact me on john.appleyard1@btinternet.com and I might have the answer.

John Appleyard
2006

Chapter 1

Why Exhibit?

It was a substantial lunch with a convivial customer. There was a good red wine and the customer insisted on buying an extra bottle. So, you, as marketing director of International Spigots, are drifting in a peaceful soporific state through the afternoon board meeting. Your mind tries to leave your body and wander away to the golf course, while Nigel, the financial director, twitters on about reducing costs by outsourcing the canteen services. Your head automatically nods in agreement, pleased that you are out of the frame for the time being. Suddenly he comes to the end of his monologue. The CEO launches in.

'Just do it, Nigel,' he snarls, then turns to you, his face animated with pent-up fury. You let out the mental clutch to engage your mind. And just in time too. His next assault is delivered at you in full battalion strength. 'Now, as you know, I've just been out to the trade fair in Hamburg. Our stand was pitiful. It was half the size of all our competitors. And we only had half our range on display. What is it with you?'

You reply lamely that, given a bigger budget, it could have been much better. And nothing had been decided until a very late stage, because of the law suit with Amalgamated Sprockets. As a result, you'd done your very best under the circumstances. He clearly isn't impressed. Your best wasn't very good.

'You've got just six months to get it right at Componex at the NEC. And I want it to be better than all our competitors this time.'

'Oh, it will be, Jason,' you say, crossing your fingers under the table. 'It will be!'

■ Exhibitions in the Grand Scheme of Things

When you have had time to reflect and calm the tremors in your knees, you realise that Jason had been more than a little unfair. Jason Barber-Browne, recently imported from Spendwise Credit Services to breathe fire into the respectable but under-performing International Spigots, was stronger on charisma than engineering experience. One of the staff can remember him as plain Jay Brown, when he used to mind his dad's dodgy CD market stall.

After a couple of weeks of new initiatives and 'new broom' cost-slashing exercises, Jason had been nicknamed 'the Argonaut', as much for his willingness to launch into heroic missions without regard for the long-term consequences, as from his name.

Maybe your assessment of the Hamburg show had been right in the first place. It was the Argonaut who wasn't thinking straight. There really hadn't been any reason for you to go onto the defensive at his tirade. You could have reminded him that none of the company's big customers or prospects bothered to travel to Hamburg. The company had nothing new to show the market. And the additional costs of space and logistics in getting everything and everybody out there for anything more ambitious would have been astronomic. In fact, logically it would have been better to have missed the show altogether. But when has logic had anything to do with being at an exhibition?

Not often, but it should.

As far as the Argonaut, who had read about international events in an airline magazine on a flight to the Big Apple, is concerned, you have to 'fly the flag'.

'Where your competitors go, you have to go. Good business sense, isn't it?'

Cobblers! Exhibitions have to pay their way, just like any other marketing activity, and generate revenue. Prestige on its own is seldom sufficient reason to exhibit.

■ Is there life without exhibiting?

There was an occasion many years ago when Ford threatened to pull out of the Motor Show. Whether they did or not in the end, I can't remember, but the point was made. The show without its biggest exhibitor was inconceivable. The Motor Show needed Ford more than Ford needed the Motor Show. Over the years, lesser marques have actually given the show a miss for a year and claimed that it made little difference to their sales. Nevertheless they nearly always returned and established their presence with something spectacular the following year.

Equally prestigious Apple Mac shows have survived without Apple's physical presence. The moral of this is that even as a major player in an industry, you don't have to be browbeaten into taking space. And if you are a lesser player and want to take on the market leaders, you don't need a presence at the big trade show to do it. Decisions have to be made on more than sentiment.

The surprising fact is that even hard-nosed business people, who would never make a media-buying decision without a sheaf of data files, will let emotion take over on exhibitions.

■ Flying the flag ... or flying in the face of logic

So that's demolished the primary reason why roughly two-thirds of companies attend trade shows. What a pity. Life is simple when you make your decision on the basis that 'We've done it for years and customers would miss us if we didn't go,' or because 'All our competitors are there and we must fly the flag.'

It's so comforting when factors like tradition and prestige can supplant all normal business responsibility. Few in management will question such fundamental sentiments (except the financial director, and what does he know about exhibitions anyway?). Venture into the morass of value and profit, and you'll never dig your way out.

That is just what I aim to do – prove that there are very practical reasons for exhibiting and that it can perform marvels for your business. And I won't even mention the past or flags.

■ Risk and Reward

If you are new to exhibiting, there is one hell of a learning curve. And if you're an old hand, you are certainly aware of the pitfalls that await at every turn to trap tyro and expert alike. It's a cliché, I know, but you never stop learning.

■ A risky business

In truth, there is nothing safe about exhibiting. My first experience of exhibitions was a miserable disaster. The show was a new one, at Earls Court, and the organisers weren't quite sure how to pitch it or who the target audience were. My MD was persuaded by a smooth-talking young salesperson that if we signed up early 'we could have the pick of the spaces'. I engaged the wrong contractor, whose ineptitude let us down at every stage, right up to the opening morning when they still hadn't finished painting. Our fascia board was stolen (we think it was our neighbours, who were also competitors, but we couldn't prove anything).

The stand design, which supposedly demonstrated the most effective approach to meeting fire regulations in public buildings, relied on a sound effects loop of roaring flames and a siren. Our neighbours objected to this except when it was turned down so low that it sounded like death-watch beetle in the woodwork. A panel fell down on the second day. To crown it all, the visitors failed to appear, as the organisers hadn't done their homework. Never again, I vowed, would I put my head on the block like that.

The sad part is that we had great ideas and a good story to tell, we planned it well and even held a training course for stand staff. It seemed that just two or three misjudgements set us spiralling out of control.

Regrettably it put me off exhibitions for years to come. I avoided them like a visit to a particularly vicious dentist, unwilling to repeat the painful experience. When I was forced into organising another stand, I did so reluctantly. Luckily I had learnt from my initial experience and have not had a bad exhibition experience since. I have become a survivor.

■ Exhibiting – a tonic for your business

However, I am always wary. No exhibitor is more than a few steps from disaster.

But if you like living on the edge, exhibiting can be enormously rewarding, not just for you, but for your company. If your company is trying to re-establish its position in an industry after a setback, there is nothing like it for results. If your sales force needs a tonic, selling in the controlled yet heady environment of an exhibition will do it. If you need a sense of perspective on how you are doing in the market, you'll soon gain it from your stand visitors.

Exhibiting is not for the faint-hearted. It is for those who want to make their mark, who want to be noticed and crave a little glory. By exhibiting, you become an exhibitionist. And if it works for you you'll never look back.

Don't lose sight of the objectives, however. Exhibiting is about increasing revenue, not about massaging egos or going to exciting places.

■ Diversity makes for interesting exhibitions

In writing this book, I hope I don't give the impression that I think I know all the answers. Indeed I don't. The suggestions I make are based on my experiences and observations of other people's successes and failures over many years. What works for me may not work for you. And indeed, exhibitions would be dull places if we all followed the same rules. Diversity of approach and thought-processes is what gives exhibitions their vitality. My ideas are set out here to help those who are floundering in an ocean of uncertainty and to stimulate those who are dissatisfied with what they are doing.

My aim is to help you to become like me, a survivor. If it helps you progress beyond being a mere survivor, that is great.

■ Not a Lot of People Know This . . .

Now for a few statistics that might surprise you. In Britain, exhibitions are among the largest of business-to-business media. Exhibitions, if we include outdoor events, account for about 11 per cent of the total media spend, more than national newspapers, and are only surpassed by television, direct mail and regional newspapers.

They are growing at a rate of about 8 per cent per annun. Not a lot of people know that. The Exhibition Venues Association, quote some pretty staggering statistics. Even if you think they might be biased, the figures still have to be heeded.

Here are some of the statistics put out by the Exhibition Venues Association:

■ Total spend on exhibitions in 2004 was estimated at £1,690 million and that figure was based on just 44 per cent of all UK exhibitions (those that take place at EVA[1]-qualifying venues). The figure was much higher in 2001 at £2,047 million, when outdoor events were included, which they are not now.
■ The number of UK exhibitions grew from 796 in 1997, to 915 in 2004, roughly a 2 per cent annual increase.
■ The number of visitors to UK exhibitions in 2004 was 9.5 million. The figure has consistently hovered round 10 million for many years. Of those exhibitions that report overseas visitors, 14.7 per cent of the visitors come from abroad.
■ Companies that exhibit at UK shows claim to spend 41 per cent of their company's annual promotional budget on an average of eight shows.

---

1 *UK Exhibition Facts*, published by the Exhibition Venues Association, 15 Keeble Court, Fairmeadows, North Seaton, Northumberland NE63 9SF, tel. +44 (0)1670 818801. Price £200 plus VAT.

- If you think that exhibiting is the preserve of the mega-rich, prepared to be gobsmacked. The average spend per exhibition stand is around just £4,500!

That's some industry! Actually, Bill Richards of EVA believes that it is wrong to call it an industry. It is so diverse and changeable. Exhibitions that were huge just ten years ago have disappeared without trace. New ones have popped up from nowhere. It's dynamic, exciting and fun.

Yet in most companies, exhibitions are regarded as the Cinderellas of marketing. They appear just above in-store merchandising and gratuities to charities in marketing plans. Where they appear on a list is immaterial. Exhibition people, like you and me, aren't precious about our trade. We know our worth. What we contribute is what matters.

■ Exhibitions as a Marketing Tool

■ What is marketing?

Maybe at this point I should establish what it is that I understand by marketing. Agreeing on a definition has taxed business gurus over the generations.

'*Maximising profit through consumer satisfaction*' comes to the fore in my brain, remembered from a college lecture long ago. Yet Boots the Chemist is the epitome of customer satisfaction in the business it knows so well. Every Boots customer knows the company and loves it for what it is. It cannot, however, diversify successfully into other areas and achieve the growth it deserves.

'*Finding latent demand and meeting that demand at a profit to the company*' is another flawed definition. There was no latent demand for McCain Frozen Chips. The 'housewife', in those politically incorrect days, had no concept of frozen chips and didn't demand them, but soon recognised a good thing when it arrived.

I would submit that to the exhibitor, marketing means '*Presenting an organisation's goods and services in such a way that a positive and profitable change in attitude and buying patterns is brought about.'* If I continue in this vein, I'll end up a marketing guru on the lecture circuit.

■ Changing attitudes

Changing behaviour is what makes companies great and successful. IKEA has changed the way we buy furniture. It didn't invent the flat-pack and it wasn't the first to make stylish furniture available to all. But it was the first retailer to combine the two and sell them in a well-planned and friendly store.

So 'change' must be the main pillar on which marketing resides. When planning exhibitions, it is worth pondering what you want that 'change' to be, and how you can best bring it about. In fact, exhibitions are excellent vehicles for changing people's attitudes.

Most people's perceptions of organisations derive from what I call 'third party' media, like print, packaging, posters and consumer programmes on the television. There is no physical contact between you, the customer, and anybody or anything from the company, until you actually buy its products.

Exhibitions are the only medium that provides first-person contact without commitment. Customers both meet suppliers in person and handle the products before they buy. These are the two most effective ways to bring about a change in attitude.

■ Branding

If 'change' is the main pillar, there is a vital buttress that prevents it from falling over, and that is 'branding'. There is no point in making something life-changing that everybody will clamour for, if they cannot recognise it when they see it. Without branding, goods become commodities and are sold purely on price.

Nothing startling there. Basic coursework stuff, in fact. But so often forgotten, especially in exhibitions. How often have you been to an exhibition with rows and rows of stands with salespeople pouring out their souls to attract your attention and convince you that their products will change your life. At the time, they seem so plausible.

Branding doesn't end with the logo. The whole design should reflect the corporate style

Then, once you've left the exhibition and are sitting on the train on the way home, you take out the sheaf of leaflets you have gathered. In how many cases can you match a leaflet to a stand and the people you talked to? Very few. The ones you do remember are either old friends and existing contacts or companies where the branding was exceptionally strong.

■ Branding to establish recall

On average, a visitor to an exhibition will probably remember in detail no more than 20 stands out of several hundred looked at. For an exhibitor who has invested £50,000 in a stand, not to feature in that list of 20 has been the waste of a lot of money. Unfortunately, exhibitors like that form the great majority. They have failed to lift their branding above the level of mashed potato.

There is only one way to ensure recall. As a marketeer, hurl in your maximum branding effort, and then some.

■ An urban myth with more than a grain of truth

We've all heard the story, possibly an urban myth, about the sales team who arrived at an exhibition to find that their stand structure had inadvertently been included in a shipment of castings to Nigeria. So they toddled round to the local repertory theatre and borrowed some flats from the scenery store. Next they contacted a signwriter to hastily scrawl their logo onto a sheet of hardboard. With the paint barely dry, they set up shop on their otherwise empty space.

Naturally, to make up for their other shortcomings, they exercised their selling skills to the full. Moreover, word got round about their misfortune and the good and generous of the exhibition world rallied to help them. The results were phenomenal. More good leads and appointments than you could shake a clipboard at.

This story is often quoted by financial directors to demonstrate that all your expensive branding is a waste of time. If they took the trouble, however, they would probably work out that the reverse is true. That sales team had branded themselves very effectively as the down-to-earth, no-nonsense, we'll-work-our-socks-off-for-you company. Customers were impressed by their salesmanship and willingness to help.

In a prestigious show where big spenders had built plywood palaces, they had been unique. Had every stand in the show been like theirs, it wouldn't have worked. Branding works, sometimes in ways we don't expect. Incidentally, that perhaps-mythical sales team is always talked of as being American, which possibly highlights one of the major differences in attitude between American exhibitors and their European counterparts: a concentration on raw selling rather than stand design and finish.

▮ Exhibitions as part of the media

It's perhaps difficult to regard exhibitions as part of the media. But, just like television advertising, press and direct mail, exhibitions provide a channel through which messages pass from you to your customers.

Continuity across the media is important. Pay great attention to those messages and ensure they are in tune with other media.

When a visitor comes onto your stand, he or she should recognise the same business story from press and television advertising.

Exhibitions are different

Exhibitions, however, have one very big difference from other media. No doubt you spotted it immediately. They provide a two-way channel for information. In addition to promoting your products, they also allow information to be passed back to you from your market.

In sales training, we learn that effective selling can be divided into 60 per cent listening, 30 per cent presentation and 10 per cent completion. An exhibition is the only promotional medium where this can be applied directly. In advertising and direct mail, the listening has to be done through the wholly artificial means of market research. An advertisement has to take an approach that best fits the majority of the target audience, ignoring any attempt to satisfy individual needs. On an exhibition stand, each visitor can be given individual attention, and their particular needs met with an individual solution.

It's a great pity that exhibition planning isn't generally approached with the attention to detail that advertising media buyers use. The criteria are very similar. Each show, like each publication or channel, has its audience profile and rate card. So you can calculate costs per thousand in exactly the same way. Real estate at a venue is valued by position, size and visibility, just as in a magazine. So it isn't difficult for you to estimate the relative attractiveness of the shows clamouring for your business. And, indeed, compare them critically with other media.

The value of the response

Some marketers might point to higher coupon return through press advertising and direct mail. I would submit that although your exhibitions may generate fewer responses, the quality of leads is much higher and they are inherently more productive.

At a three-day trade show, your sales staff have one-on-one contact with more people than they are likely to meet in three months of tramping round their territory. Many of those people will be new prospects that would never normally have been approached or customers that are difficult to reach under other circumstances.

A survey in the USA estimated that at an average exhibition, over 80 per cent of visitors to a stand were unknown to the stand staff. One can of course question the quality of the leads generated, but if just a quarter of them prove to be potential customers, that could double your sales database in one hit.

Moreover, your staff will have on hand the full range of marketing tools to back them up, as well as senior staff to call upon for support – if they can be prised away from the heady atmosphere of press conferences and trade federation receptions.

■ A perfect selling environment

A well-planned stand will provide a perfect selling environment for your sales personnel. If they find it too restricting, there is always the bar to resort to for revitalising the selling organs. There is nothing like a busy stand, with enthusiastic sales staff working their socks off, for stimulating the adrenal glands. It becomes a buzzing microcosm of the company, a place that is a metaphor for the vitality and drive of the organisation. If it doesn't look that way on yours, something's definitely wrong.

■ Consumer shows

Consumer shows like the Motor Show, the Ideal Home Exhibition and the Boat Show are somewhat different from the trade shows most of us go to, with their restricted and specialist audiences. Consumer shows are seen almost as a form of sponsored entertainment. For most people, going to a consumer show is an experience, just like going to a museum or sporting event. They are unlikely to spend much money at the Motor Show, preferring to wonder and dream. Having said that, the exhibitions play an important part in the exhibitor's marketing strategy. While we are all potential car buyers, we don't place our orders on the Ford stand for the newest Mondeo variant. Indeed, many cars on display are concept cars, not even available for purchase. The show is about image, branding and supporting dealer networks.

The Ideal Home Exhibition is in complete contrast. Here, although there are large exhibits mainly for display, visitors can buy a wide array of products, just as in a market, with stand-holders hawking their wares. They can also place orders for furniture, double glazing and garage doors if they wish, or buy kitchen knives and things for sealing plastic bags, straight from the salespeople.

The Boat Show is different again. The vessels exhibited have a value equal to any capital goods at trade shows, but stand-holders are more than willing to take orders on the spot from private buyers. Indeed, although there is a business market through yacht and boat charter companies, their orders placed at the show will not compare with the volume of private orders.

All the companies who attend these exhibitions do so as part of a carefully planned marketing strategy. For many manufacturers, especially where other media cannot do the products justice, exhibiting is the prime source of orders.

Impressive as consumer shows are, still the bulk of exhibitions will be trade fairs. By far the majority of exhibitors are targeting trade customers. So most of this book will be devoted to trade stands.

■ 'Your Competitors Will Be There . . .'

'And here will be Allied Grubscrews.' Brian, the salesman for Componex points a bitten nail at one of the most prominent blocks of red felt-tipping on the exhibition plan. It looks like a subcontinent on a pre-war map of the British Empire. 'Right by the entrance, 900 square metres. Now I've been keeping this super space opposite them just for you. Sorry they got in first with the prime site – the one the punters see immediately they come in – but that's the way it goes. The one I've reserved for you is bigger.'

He points again. You're looking at a skinny oblong cross-hatched in pencil on the plan. It's facing the wrong way, is long and narrow and only has one side open to the aisle. So what if it is bigger? A big space in the wrong place is about as useful as a garden centre in the middle of the Sahara.

■ Big isn't always beautiful

This business of trying to out-space your competitors is very compelling, especially when you have Jason the Argonaut impressing on you that bigger is more beautiful. As we've already seen, he looks upon it all as a matter of personal prestige, an aid to his corporate social climbing. It's his ego that counts when he lords it at the stand with his cronies. He comes for that awards ceremony that every organiser conveniently seems to bolt on to an exhibition. And the stand is a personal theatre where he can deliver his monologue about last year's awards being 'a fix'. Even if it was six months before he'd joined.

The brown-nosed marketer will probably book a stand way beyond the company's needs just to placate a boss like Jason. The boss will pat our marketer on the back when he learns that the space will be even bigger than Allied Grubscrews. With any luck, once that marketer has scratched his mark on the order, the Argonaut will not normally enquire whether that enormous, ill-shaped bit of real estate rented for three days will be a paying concern. On the other hand, he just might.

Realistically you rarely get what you really want. We all appreciate that exhibition organisers have to live, and theirs is a particularly tough way to earn a crust. Even Allied Grubscrews will have been put under pressure to reserve the prime site by a persuasive salesman who probably told them that you were very interested in it. 'Snap it up quickly, or lose it to Spigots,' he said. So snap it up they did.

■ Put yourself in a visitor's shoes

Don't be pressurised by the salesperson. Take the plan and consider the options creatively. Think like a visitor to the show.

Visualise the hall in your mind's eye. If you can think in 3D, so much the better.

What would you do when you first enter the hall? Which way would you walk? What would take your eye? It's not always the first or biggest stand that attracts you. In fact, visitors often look beyond the first one they encounter. Among the bombardment of information, they certainly remember more of what they see and hear on the last stand visited than the first. How to be last stand visited? Well, I'll come to that later.

■ Learn from retailers

One useful exercise is to observe the behaviour of shoppers in a shopping mall. Few shoppers buy from the first shop they visit, unless they know exactly what they want. They prefer to compare quality, style and price from several outlets. Frequently they will buy from the last shop in sheer desperation.

When they enter shops they display recognisable patterns of behaviour. Always assuming that you don't have your groceries delivered by Fortnum & Mason, you too will subconsciously dance to the retailer's tune. The shopper in a supermarket has objectives – the items on the shopping list, mostly staples. On the way to those necessary purchases, all purposely stacked far away from the entrance of the store, the route is lined with attractive goods that the shopper doesn't really need, but are more profitable for the retailer.

Observe the traffic flows and which areas receive the greatest 'footfall'. Notice that, while shoppers appear to be looking ahead, their peripheral vision becomes very sensitive and they deviate from the obvious route. Some are attracted by goods marked 'cheap', while others veer towards those marked 'new' or 'exclusive'.

While we all have the same basic nutritional needs, we choose different ways to satisfy them, plus we have some discretionary disposable income to dispose of along the way. Retailers plan their shops accordingly.

In effect, an exhibition is like a shopping mall, with big and small shops situated to take advantage of visitors' tastes and spending power. In time you will learn to read an exhibition site plan critically and be able to spot graveyard spaces to avoid and the bargains that others have failed to recognise.

I will show you later how we can all learn from retailers when planning our stands.

■ Negotiate hard

However, you don't need to be an expert to become the hard-nosed negotiator. Just prepare your ground and stick to your guns. How much do you really want to spend? How much business will you get from this show? How will it stimulate sales between this and the next Componex? If you do your homework, even Jason the Argonaut in a wildly expansive mood won't be able to dent your arguments.

And remember one simple fact – a visitor is more likely to trade with the last stand he visits than the first. And he'll certainly remember it better.

■ Mission Impossible – or Possible?

'Your mission, and you have no option but to accept it, is to increase sales revenue by 12 per cent over the coming fiscal year.' You wake from the ghastly nightmare as the tape self-destructs in your ashtray. You reach to shut off the alarm and you realise with relief that you are not Tom Cruise and you aren't being asked to enter your competitor's office through the air conditioning duct.

■ What a 12 per cent increase in sales really means

However, part of the dream is true. You have been tasked with raising sales by 12 per cent. As you make that early morning cup of tea you ponder the problem. Perhaps 12 per cent isn't so bad. It could have been worse.

Think again. The 12 per cent gain is an aggregate figure. It expects you to compensate for lost business as well as attracting new business.

Your company loses at least 10 per cent of its customers each year to competition. Five per cent is irretrievably lost to changes in technology and to customers going out of business. And the market is declining by 3 per cent per annum. So that means having to improve performance, not by 12 per cent, but by 30 per cent. It's beyond the capability of mortal man, even Jason.

■ A ray of hope

Advertising, that's it! More space. A new campaign. But then again, the space costs have just gone up, so it might have to be less space rather than more. A new campaign won't solve the problem. The current one is a cracker and is just getting into its stride. Unless you are advertising fantastic offers or drastically slashing prices, advertising takes time. As you sip your tea, your mind runs through the options. None will give instant results.

Then it hits you. Your sole ray of hope.

You've just signed up for Componex, in three months' time. Give credit where it is due. The Argonaut was right about that. But it should be examined critically as a marketing exercise, not just satisfying Jason's whim.

Is the seemingly impossible possible after all? Can an exhibition stand raise sales to the extent you need? First let's look at where that 30 per cent will have to come from.

■ Customer retention

You might be able to reduce the haemorrhage of business from its current 18 per cent by demonstrating that you are offering a better deal and are adopting new technology. Could the stand help here? It could feature the new imported, better value lines that will appeal to the disloyal customers and at the same time address the technology issues. These are not products that you wish to feature in your advertising, because to put it bluntly they don't fit your new trendy image. Put that down for 8 per cent.

How much can your sales force improve existing customer retention and development? Hardly any under current conditions, your salespeople will tell you. They are doing their utmost. There aren't enough hours in the day, they claim. Naturally you suspect the sales force are spending far too much time calling on their old buddies and insufficient on chasing new business. But when you look at the orders coming in from those existing accounts, do they reflect the full potential of each customer, or is the customer just 'keeping you sweet' with minimum, but acceptable, orders?

■ The value of exhibiting to existing customers

The stand would help immeasurably in such a situation. You would have the full range of products on display, maybe a demonstration of the newest line and a board-level director on hand. The salespeople will have support like they never get in the field. And it doesn't end there. Most customers visiting the show will be represented not just by their buyers, but also by all senior decision-makers. It's your one chance to meet the person who really gives the thumbs up. With these advantages, your stand staff should surely achieve a further 15 per cent from your existing customer base.

■ Adding value

There is a new and fashionable way of squeezing more from your existing customers – adding value. I'm sure you're only too familiar with the principle. If you extend your contribution along the value chain, possibly through additional services, each addition to the contract yields more revenue with hardly any incremental selling cost. Also, adding value binds the customer closer to you. With the full range of goods and services on display, there will never be a better chance to discuss a deal. However, adding value warrants a book in itself, and a great many have indeed been written on the subject.

■ There is always new business you aren't aware of

All that new business that your sales force swears isn't really out there, but you know is, will be at the show. And the show gives you the finest opportunity you will ever have to evaluate its quality and quantity.

Believe me, however well you know your market, there is always somebody out there with a potential big order that you don't know about. There will be other people who are contemplating diversification and need help with setting up new operations. There are companies being taken over, where the new incumbents are eager to negotiate with fresh suppliers in the hope of reducing costs.

Every market is fluid, which salespeople in the field with set call schedules often fail to appreciate. If they do appreciate the changes, they are often wary of leaving their comfort zones. Those potential new customers will pass your stand. If you can only make them stop for a talk, you have the best opportunity you will ever have of getting an appointment. A 7 per cent increase from this potential new business shouldn't be out of the question.

■ Mission possible

Bingo – 30 per cent! If it were that simple, you wouldn't have to do anything except organise exhibitions.

Unfortunately, there is a snag. Although exhibitions can lead you towards these results, few actual sales are made at the average trade stand. Exhibitions are just part of a marketing mix in which all parts support each other.

The final deal is made after much deliberation and negotiation. I shall discuss this further shortly.

It's like hooking a fish. Although there's a more than even chance that you will catch it, you are not assured of a supper until it's in the boat.

■ Effort in, rewards out

An exhibition is the one marketing activity where you are in absolute control and where any extra effort put in should produce results. Mind you, it will be hard graft. The difference between this and most other marketing exercises that involve you and your staff is that here you will have to do much of the work yourselves. There is no market research company to do the fieldwork. No advertising agency to work out a convenient media schedule for you to rubber stamp. No promotions company to send out hundreds of samples from a handling house in Warrington. No call centre in Calcutta. You can't latch a couple of questions on to one of those massive consumer surveys. It's just you and your team. You are on your own and you feel very exposed. On the other hand, there is nobody to hold you back.

Even with everything in your favour, your commitment to the task will be tested time after time as things go wrong and hard decisions have to be made right up to the end. If you are short-tempered or lack a sense of humour, recruit somebody to take the burden off you.

You will by now be aware of the tremendous effort and cost of building the stand and staffing it for a week. If you are new to the job, the first thing you should do is find out the extent of the commitment from those with relevant experience, or you will be in for a shock.

■ Return on investment (ROI)

So your exhibition stand might be the key to meeting that seemingly impossible target. But you need more than gut instinct to justify it. Working out if the stand will give an acceptable ROI is not easy, but you have to do it.

■ What is the marketing pay-off from a stand?

At most trade shows few orders are actually signed, and if they are, the signing ceremony will have been set up by PR people long beforehand for the trade press. How, then, do sales actually result from all this effort?

Many exhibitors will tell you that you can't expect to achieve anything beyond collecting names of prospects for future use. So is a stand's function just to generate sales leads for use after the show is over?

Surely not. I believe there must be more to it than that. I'm convinced it's about initiating the sales process. Sometimes all you will get is a name, address and an indication of the prospect's level of interest. But if your sales team are doing their job, they'll progress beyond just getting leads, and push to book appointments. If they are even smarter, they'll arrange a date for a prospect's visit to your factory. Smarter still and they'll get you on a tender list or secure an invitation to write a proposal.

The sale of industrial goods is a smooth process that should progress from initial contact seamlessly to completion. It shouldn't be segmented into discrete stages, which give the customer an opportunity to have second thoughts. On the stand let the process flow as far as possible and get commitment to a positive action beyond the point it reaches. That positive action must include a date and a place when contact will be made.

■ More about customer retention

Most of the people who are fixated by merely collecting new leads ignore the tremendous value a stand can have in customer retention and extension of existing business. When existing customers arrive, what do you do? Of course, you welcome them courteously and chat amiably about levels of business and exchange industry gossip. Trading, they say, is getting tougher. You sympathise. Then one of two things will happen. The customer is either escorted off to the bar to chat over old times or invited to take a seat and offered a cup of coffee. Sometimes a proper business meeting results, but that happens far too rarely. Usually, after a little while, the customer moves on and little has been achieved except an exchange of pleasantries.

I have watched bemused many times while strong buying signals are totally ignored. In other circumstances, they would have been instantly recognised. It seems that few really capitalise on the opportunities afforded by the undivided attention of a customer on your turf.

Apart from the benefits of extending good relations and selling on, you should recognise the dangers posed by a less than friendly reception. A curt remark or insufficient attention to a valued customer will play instantly into your competitors' hands. You probably won't even notice the slight. You can bet your life that the customer who visits your stand will also visit your competitors. And they will be waiting in predatory mood to welcome him or her into their den-like chat areas.

■ Projected sales, an unrealistic target

So it's unrealistic to set projected sales as your objective. I've heard this done many times and it leads to disappointment. You just can't say that, from any given level of activity, you can predict £1.3 million to result. There are just too many variables between that meeting on the stand and signing the contract. Nevertheless, sales in the period following the exhibition are a measure of the stand's effectiveness, especially when compared with previous years.

■ Objectives and 'productive contacts'

What objectives should you set for the show? Of course, it varies with the products you sell. If you are Airbus Industries, the value of your stand at Farnborough and the Paris Air Show will take some time to manifest itself. It undoubtedly plays a significant role, but it would be very difficult to untangle its effect from all the other promotional activities and political pressures.

If you are a conventional industrial supplier, you should be reaping the reward three months after an exhibition. This is the time needed for leads to be converted into appointments, and those appointments to be booked into tenders or specifications. At this point the residual effect of the exhibition tails off and hard selling takes over (see Figure 1).

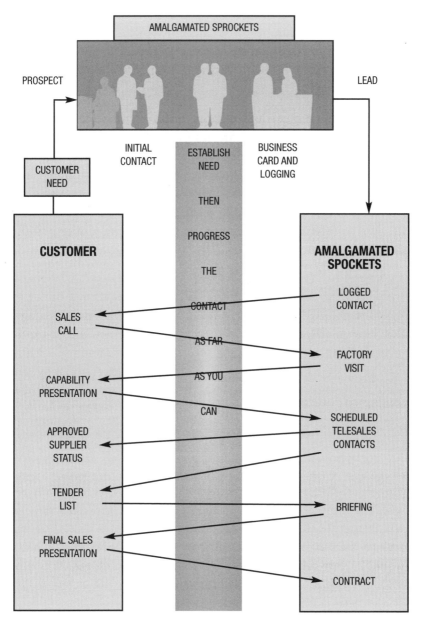

Figure 1 Chain of events initiated by contact on an exhibition stand.

So I suggest that the objectives set for the presence at an exhibition should be a given number of sales appointments or presentations and a given number of resulting sales opportunities. I like to call these 'productive contacts', and they can be graded in terms of quality and value.

When drawing up objectives, I like to construct a matrix of 'productive contacts', with columns for anticipated revenue and rows for the stage of sale attained, ranging from existing business secured, through lead, appointment to tender or pitch. The most important point about objectives is that they should be attainable and all involved should be committed to them.

■ You have to work harder with new business for the same return

Is it possible to relate those objectives into revenue terms? I think it is, although one has to be careful. If your sales force have done their job well, they will have secured a number of new leads, a proportion of which will be marginal.

New customers tend not to yield as much revenue on each order as existing customers. You will have to fight harder to grab the business from a tried and trusted supplier, often with lower margins. The more new leads your sales staff generate, the greater will be the proportion of marginal ones. The old 80:20 rule applies here – 80 per cent of new business opportunity will come from 20 per cent of leads.

The orders on these new accounts will often be smaller to start with, as new customers will probably not be keen to shift all their business in one go and will probably engage you initially on a 'trial run'. You may also have to extend greater credit than you would like, on what is probably a greater risk.

■ Direct selling from stands

Of course, some stands don't worry about productive contacts. Staff actually roll up their sleeves and sell products directly over the counter. You can pick these stands out instantly. Brash as a mail order catalogue, they dispense with subtle graphics and cosy chat areas. They need every inch of space for warehousing, counters and tills. T-shirts, kitchen knives, motor accessories, computer software, mobile phones and petfood. These are living proof that stands can sell.

■ No Limits?

Just how much business can be initiated from a trade exhibition stand? Wouldn't it be great to say that the sky's the limit? The harder you work, the more your reward. Sorry, I'm afraid it doesn't work like that. There are physical constraints on how much new activity any stand can generate. This is determined by its size and the duration of the show.

■ How much business can you handle?

Let's take, for example, last year's International Spigots' stand at Componex. You managed to keep three sales staff, two hostesses and a receptionist on the stand permanently, and a director present for much of the time. The show lasted three days and was open eight hours a day. You could discount the first and last two hours of the show. Very little selling took place then. Each salesperson was allowed an hour for lunch. This meant that each salesperson sold for a total of 17 hours. Allowing about eight minutes for each contact, this equated to a maximum of seven contacts per hour per person. The maximum number of contacts possible to these three stalwarts during the show was therefore around 360.

They did well in practice by attaining 315, of which 60 were graded A in quality. That is, capable of yielding viable orders and open to approach within six months. In addition, the director took on a further 20 VIP visitors, which secured four concrete orders and eight promises. The hostesses performed beyond expectations. Although they were hired-in staff, they soon got the hang of things and joined in active selling on day two to generate a further 14 grade A productive contacts and 30 grade B contacts. Then there were two intervening evenings, both used to entertain existing customers and secure business.

In fact, everybody excelled. Overall, 74 high-grade productive contacts from the troops is better than most stands of that size make. It may not sound a lot, but 20 per cent converted to orders within a year, yielding a revenue of £2.6 million. The profit on those sales was £650,000. The gross cost of the stand was £135,000. Additional selling costs amounted to £85,000. I would say this was an acceptable return, wouldn't you?

■ Can you improve?

Everything can be improved. But can you physically increase productive contacts by the much needed 30 per cent at this year's Componex? Like every ambitious target, it can only be achieved if additional resources are allocated.

Increased efficiency can give you marginal improvements. Sales managers tend to resort to the traditional means of increasing productivity – stick and carrot. But you just can't do it by pep talks to the stand staff. Undoubtedly, their effectiveness can be enhanced through training and possibly incentives. But there are just so many people they can physically talk to in an hour, even if you promised them a Ferrari apiece.

■ Bigger and better

The increases demanded from on high have to be achieved through scaling up all round. The stand will probably have to be bigger to give the capacity to make more contacts. If you've already booked the space, you'll either have to renegotiate with the organisers for more or ditch something on the stand that takes up space.

■ Objectives for non-profit-making concerns

If you are not a commercial profit-making organisation, don't think all this does not apply. Even charities and government information services need objectives. You presumably have a strong message to convey so it's worthwhile contacting a sample of your stand visitors after the show to find out what they learnt and how you could do it better. You may not need your productive contacts to buy from you, but you do require them to perform some action, and here are a few that I have been involved with.

- Gaining membership for an organisation.
- Lobbying on behalf of a pressure group or trade association.
- Getting the public to visit a place or event.
- Increasing awareness of a public information website or helpline.
- Informing the public about a new piece of legislation.
- Recruiting staff or offering career advice.

All of these can have quantifiable objectives. Set them before the show and monitor by questionnaire or phone call afterwards.

■ And the Rest

If the prime reason for exhibiting is yielding productive contacts, can your exhibition stand perform any other uses? Provided they don't impede the prime function, yes. In fact, other stand uses should support and enhance the selling activity. However, they should do so in ways that don't drag your stand sales staff away from their primary task, which is to deal with customers. Where other functions require people task, those people should be engaged and budgeted for separately.

There are lots of immeasurable benefits offered by a well-designed stand:

- Being the stage for press opportunities.
- A general increase in brand awareness by visitors.
- Moving volumes of literature from your storeroom, where it achieves nothing, into customer filing cabinets, where it can be called upon when a need arises.

Indeed, in addition to generating productive contacts, most exhibitors try to combine a number of other tasks. I've seen these listed as stand objectives by clients:

- Making a memorable statement about the company, its brands and its products (branding again).
- Launching a new range of products or a new initiative.
- Providing a comfortable and well-equipped arena in which to present the product range, negotiate a deal or entertain VIPs.
- Demonstrating complex products to quite large audiences.
- Introducing the company to a new market.

Yes, there are many secondary reasons for having a stand, but don't lose sight of the first one.

■ Horses for Courses

Wait a minute! Impressive stands in prime sites aren't relevant to small companies with hardly two credit cards to rub together, I hear you cry. Don't tell me, this fits you to a tee.

And all this talk about missions! The main one for many is just getting there and set up. Then, if you've got little more than the small cash in your back pocket to spend, is there anything worthwhile that can be done when all the resources you can throw at it are a briefcase, a box of brochures and a laptop? More important, if it can be done, will it be effective?

■ Hey, small spender!

To start with, not all exhibitions are on the scale of the Motor Show. Many are local and even some that are international are so specialised that they attract a small number of stand-holders on tiny budgets. In fact, by far the majority of exhibitors are small spenders. They must be if the Exhibition Venues Association figures are to be believed. The EVA claims that the average expenditure per stand is £4,500. Bearing in mind there are some very big players, there must also be many very small ones.

Most major exhibitions have large areas for the less affluent, and often these are the most interesting and enjoyable. Certainly they are the friendliest.

If you aren't a big spender, you shouldn't feel inferior. Even large companies book small stands at shows where they can't justify a high investment but like to have a presence. What's more, small stands aren't necessarily less effective than large ones. It all depends on what you hope to achieve.

■ Shell schemes

If cash and capabilities are a real problem, the organisers will help you by providing what is called a 'shell scheme'. This supplies all your basic needs, like walls, ceiling, carpet, electricity, a fascia with your company name on it and possibly simple lighting. All you have to do is provide the furniture and fittings. Often the organisers will send you a catalogue of these, so that you can hire directly from them. You are assured that everything you order will be there on the day before opening. Great, they're doing all the hard graft and giving you a fixed price for doing it.

Of course, you've spotted the disadvantage immediately. All the stands look the same, and for the sake of providing something that goes with everybody's corporate colours, the carpets and furniture are in boring old battleship grey, or as they poetically term it, pale charcoal.

■ Making a statement with a shell stand

To make your 5m × 3m box distinctive is where your flair and imagination comes in. You don't have to accept the standard furniture. You can put whatever you like, within reason, into your little domain. You can cover their uniform grey lining with as many graphic panels as you can cram in. We've all seen television programmes like *Changing Rooms*, where a mundane, tired little room, probably about the same size as your stand, is transformed into a dramatic fashion statement. The teams are allowed a few hundred pounds to bring this about. You can do the same with about the same expenditure.

Stand-holders have created tropical beaches with a few bags of sand and potted palms, Egyptian tombs with painted flats and a few props from the local auction room, and penthouse flats using large panoramic wall coverings.

■ Modular systems

When you've tired of shell schemes and want to move on, there are modular systems. These are big versions of Meccano or Lego. Here you hire a kit of parts and a bag of tools, together with a chappie in a T-shirt and baseball cap who knows how it all fits together. He'll tell you this is the first stepping stone in his career to becoming a roadie with a major band.

This system gives you more flexibility, but still costs less than starting from scratch. If you have a schedule of several exhibitions throughout the year, you might even consider buying the system and hiring another chappie to look after it.

Modular systems are available at every level of sophistication and complexity. In their simplest form, such systems are no more than a series of flat panels held together with clips. These are so basic that, to make them free-standing, you have to use return panels and braces, or zigzag each section. At their most sophisticated, they employ advanced aluminium extrusions that either slot directly into one another or use proprietary connectors. The top-end systems allow amazing structures to be built with a hi-tech look.

■ Pop-up units

Another system makes it even simpler. These are 'pop-up' units. They are made in the form of a clever metal structure that comes out of a tub-shaped carrying case and expands into a curved wall before your very eyes. It does everything it says on the tub.

You then attach graphics panels by one of a number of methods. In theory, you should be able to erect the structure in about 15 minutes. In practice, while the metal structure rarely presents problems, there always seems to be a design fault with the panel fixings. Originally pop-ups were intended for those booths that you see at railway stations, motorway pull-ins or college reception areas. They are unpretentious and convenient, and, with well-designed graphics, can look rather smart. The idea, and it shows how long they have been about, was devised so that they could be carried about in the boots of Ford Sierras.

The manufacturers of these systems realised, however, that owners might want to progress to something more adventurous and have devised extensions and accessories. They have even introduced methods of bolting several units together. So now you can have curvy blocks and sweeping walls. To be fair, while amazing effects can be created, one can't help feeling that the original pleasing simplicity has been lost.

■ Purpose-built stands

Even purpose-built stands need not cost the earth. But a word of warning. Don't compromise on quality. The show may last only three days, but the structure will take quite a hammering from the constant flow of visitors. Talk to a recognised stand contractor experienced in structures, cabling, finishes and coverings. If you're short of cash, the contractor may have parts of other people's discarded stands stored on the premises. These can often be revamped into something presentable. Other or fascinating items may also be available like Greek pillars, Concorde nosecones or giant Oscars. If you feel so inclined, he could probably knock you up a Formula 1 pit lane or the Cabinet Room at Number 10.

■ Just Like Shopping

I mentioned earlier about studying traffic flows in a supermarket. You might also liken an exhibition to a shopping mall. There are large stands and small ones. Some are promoting big complex products or product ranges, while others are selling components. Yet others are concerned with support services. The main difference is that the exhibition lasts only a matter of days. This means that exhibitors have less opportunity to learn than retailers do. Retail outlets survive because they have hit on a winning formula and they can monitor its performance day by day. You would do well to take a look at how they do it. It could save you disappointment.

■ Branding

What do you notice when you first enter the shopping mall? Each shop is instantly recognisable, not just from its fascia, but from its colour scheme, its style of window display and it general ambience. That is branding. The branding also says much about the type of outlet – whether it is up or downmarket, the type of goods sold and the age of its target market. When you enter the shop, the branding continues through everything on show, from the carpet to the uniforms of the assistants. It all sends out a consistent message. Bear that in mind when planning your stand.

■ Multi-sensory appeal

The second thing you will probably notice is that retailers try to appeal to as many senses as possible and in the most direct way possible. They don't cover their walls with big display boards with long, wordy descriptions of the goods. They show the goods themselves, and, if the goods aren't available, they use pictures. They know their customers have limited attention spans.

If possible, the goods are touchable. When we handle products, it stimulates a feeling of 'ownership'. If we like them, we bond with the goods and we feel we want to take them away with us. There are subtle (and sometimes less subtle) sounds to soothe and relax us. Lighting is very important, bright when it needs to accentuate, soft when it needs to coerce. The lighting scheme provides depth and interest. The outlet may even resort to aromatherapy. How many stands get anywhere near this level of customer engagement?

■ Allowing adequate space

Most importantly, retailers make adequate space for the customer to circulate and will probably have thought deeply about traffic flows. Some garish sale goods are placed at the entrance to entice shoppers inside, then other more serious sales goods are positioned next to premium lines so that the shopper is encouraged to look at both and compare qualities. Counters do not dominate the shop floor, as they come into play after the shopper has made a choice. Every inch is planned to make it easy for the customer to select, feel and try the goods.

■ Staff behaviour

Watch also the behaviour of good shop staff. Ever helpful, but never in the way. They don't discourage shoppers by 'swooping' on us when we are merely looking with little intention of buying. When a customer shows interest, they enquire if they can help without being overtly pushy. And when confronted with troublesome or argumentative customers, they defuse the situation pleasantly.

Shops are great role models for exhibition stands. Isn't it a shame that exhibitors don't pay attention to them? In the shop the customer is always king. At exhibitions the customer is treated more like a peasant. Many stands are ruled by groups of suited yobbos, joking and ogling passers by in a way that would never be tolerated in a shopping mall.

There are valuable lessons for all of us who exhibit if we take the trouble to observe our local Next or Boots. And it costs us nothing.

■ Show Biz

So far, it all sounds like hard work. Well, that's true, it is. But exhibiting should also be fun. One thing to remember above all is that whatever the stress and pressure, building a stand is not a matter of life or death. There will not be global disaster if your logo has been painted slightly off colour, you run out of literature or a panel falls over when somebody leans on it. Probably nobody outside your staff will notice. Everyone has their own problems.

You put right the damage and continue. Barring earthquakes, giant meteorites and alien invasion, the show must go on.

And show it is. Once your stand is erected, you are in the entertainment business. You have your auditorium. You have an audience. And you have a story to tell. Let it be told.

Chapter 2

An Exhibition Strategy

This is all tedious stuff, and I could almost forgive you for skipping these sections, if they weren't so important. Bear with me, heed my advice, and I promise life will be easier in the long run.

■ Planning Ahead

We have considered the possibility of a company attending one major trade show a year. Many do just that, but others have a busy schedule of events spread throughout the calendar. Whatever the scale of exhibiting, it is wise to plan ahead and have a strategy for your activities. Sounds obvious, doesn't it? You'd be surprised at how many otherwise rational companies seem to lose all sense of reason where exhibitions are concerned.

■ False economies

Consider this typical example. The Vice President Marketing of a well-known company has decided to attend just one show, the same as last year. Because, as always, there is a squeeze on costs, a revamp of the old stand seems the only option. A change of corporate ID hasn't helped, and all graphic elements have to be redesigned and produced. The revamp proves almost as expensive as starting from scratch, as various vital elements have already been recycled or lost. Nevertheless, the selected exhibition proves a success and the stand is put into retirement once more.

Then an opportunity arises to attend a new show in Okinawa, where space is expensive and the old stand would be far too big. It has to be cut down to a size where the original design doesn't work very well. Never mind, there isn't time to do anything new. So the work is done and the sections shipped to Japan.

The Human Resources (HR) department then decides to do a milk run of universities and asks to borrow the display boards and the company video on their return from the Far East. Off these go, in the charge of somebody on work experience who doesn't appreciate that they cost £8,000. When they arrive back with moustaches and tankards drawn in by undergraduates, they are fit only for the dustbin.

Then, to cap it all, the financial director wants to stage an event for analysts in one of the London livery halls. The original stand is no longer available, as it was scrapped in Japan to save the expense of bringing it home. A modular system is hired. The display boards are redone, but after they are complete, the director wants changes made. Overall bill £15,000.

■ Could it happen to you?

It couldn't happen in your company, could it? Bet your life it could. It happens every day and it keeps exhibition contractors in expensive 4×4s with tinted windows. All of these needs should have been foreseen and allowed for. The result is that the company has spent a fortune unnecessarily and at each stage had to make do with second best. Just think ahead. Ask around to find out what your colleagues might need when planning.

Every event that you become involved in should have a purpose, objectives, a budget and a production schedule. These should be decided at the start of the year, just like any other media plan, with possibly a small contingency to allow you to take advantage of unforeseen opportunities. That's it, no more.

■ Do only what you are certain of

When planning, be ruthless. If you aren't at least 75 per cent convinced by an option, scrap it out of hand. Only go to exhibitions where you are sure of success, no matter what the company politics demand. One good show is worth three almost good shows. It's the same as with any other business decision-making. Be decisive. Be tough.

■ Never underfund a project

If you can't afford to do it properly, don't bother doing it all. There is nothing like an exhibition for exposing yourself to the world. Your customers, competitors and the press are all looking for signs of weakness. As you stand there, with notices telling visitors to 'mind the wet paint' or a graphic panel with an unmissable spelling mistake in the headline that makes it almost pornographic (yes, I've been there), you are naked to the scorn of all who envy your success or want to get even with you. Don't ever give them that opportunity.

■ Get total commitment

As well as adequate funding, you must have conviction and commitment from all involved. Don't go ahead with something you don't think will work, just because it has cost you a fortune to get thus far. You must know of multinationals who hate their logos, but would never admit to the fact because everybody has read in *Marketing Week* that a top design company charged them a cool two million for the rebranding. The executives smile and defend the indefensible, rather than appear gullible. To make anything a success, your heart must be in it.

■ Budgeting

Yeah, you know all about budgeting, don't you? It comes up once a year and it's a pain in the backside. Normally you will set your overall budget or somebody will set it for you. If not set in stone, it will be cast in a reasonably unmalleable similar substance. It certainly won't expand to do anything unforeseen beyond minor tweaks. And you can bet your bottom dollar that it won't let you do half what you want to do, let alone satisfy the Argonaut's ego.

Budgeting exhibitions is merely a matter of working backwards from what you are allowed to spend to meet what you want to do, with a bit of creativity thrown in. That's the theory. But if you think that's simple, wait till you try.

A warning here. Don't be tempted to hide costs in other budgets, at least when you are budgeting for your own use. There's no point in fooling yourself. It's not worth it.

■ Things to include in your budget

When you start, you'll possibly jot down about five or six headings, but when you think a little deeper the list grows alarmingly. The major items you might include are:

- The cost of space in the exhibition hall (to which can be added services like electricity, plumbing, security patrols and the like).
- Stand design, construction and transport.
- Stand storage, servicing and refurbishment.
- Graphics and models.
- Electronics, such as work stations.
- Carpets, fittings, furniture and flowers.
- Staffing – include not only hired staff, but the cost of taking your own staff off the road.
- Marketing the stand – invitations, advertising in show programme, posters.
- Accommodation for staff and stand builders.
- Presenters and live elements.
- Specially produced videos.
- Merchandising and giveaways.
- Additional print requirements – brochures, leaflets and flyers that you will have to order over and above normal stock.
- Website, if you run one, to promote your presence at the show.
- PR and press packs.
- Photography.
- Prizes.
- Food and drink.

- Expenses.
- Travel to and from the show, and to and from the hotel.
- Site services like security and cleaning.
- Couriers.
- Gratuities.

Keep control of staff costs

The list seems endless. And you can no doubt see horrible grey clouds settling over some items. How, for instance, do you estimate expenses, knowing that salespeople will raid their mini-bars and treat themselves to expensive Chinese meals on your expense account? One solution is through 'per diems'. These are flat rate daily allowances given to each person to cover all out of pocket expenses. Make them quite generous, and your staff won't take advantage.

Opportunity costs

Most companies call in their sales teams for all or part of the exhibition period. While this makes a good deal of sense, it's always tempting to ignore the cost of the time taken off normal selling. Yes, they are selling product on your stand, but they are not performing their normal sales function. Since you will no doubt want credit for sales generated on the stand, it is only fair to write off their lost time against your exhibition budget. It may be necessary to offer a token to compensate for loss of commission, but most salespeople quickly realise that if the stand is well run, they will more than make up through new business.

Collateral costs

Collaterals, like print, can be hidden in some other marketing budget, but who are you fooling? The object of doing a proper budget is to satisfy yourself on the viability of exhibiting at the exhibition. Put it all in.

Gratuities

Gratuities may seem an afterthought. In this country, an odd tip to reward a doorman or cleaner is neither here nor there. Abroad, where in some countries bribery is a way of life, a substantial tip may be necessary to get things through customs or into the exhibition hall. A backhander could turn out to be a payment for something little short of a protection racket, whereby if you don't pay, accidents happen. Mostly it is just equipment that is at risk, but I have heard of threats of violence in some more questionable parts of the world.

■ Costs for exhibiting overseas

If you are exhibiting abroad, costs rapidly escalate. Not only do you have to consider travel, but there are bound to be a number of unforeseen charges. Remember that outside the UK, you are the foreigner and the cards are stacked against you. Merely being in a foreign country makes you vulnerable to overcharging and a target for scams. Somehow the day before the opening of a show is always a public holiday that nobody bothers to mention and all the carpenters and electricians have gone to the beach. Those that can be enticed back not only demand triple wages but clearly wish they were somewhere else.

■ Couriers

Make a healthy allowance for couriers. There always seems to be something heavy that is left behind and must be delivered urgently. Whatever deadline you set, print always contrives to arrive just as the exhibition van has left, and it's a mighty heavy item to send by UPS or Interlink.

■ Contingencies for a full programme

Budgeting for a number of shows may not be much more difficult than budgeting for one, as many items will require a one-off consideration. However, it is as well to build in a healthy contingency on a full programme, as towards the end of a season complacency tends to set in. Things wear out and unforeseen changes have to be made. It is always on the last outing that damage to the stand occurs and vital components get lost. Sod's Law is rampant in the exhibition business.

■ Storage

With a programme of shows throughout the year, you must make allowance for what happens to the stand and equipment when not on site. The contractor will store it for you at a price, but often his facilities are not ideal. Also, don't be surprised if bits get 'borrowed'. I grumble when this happens, but not too hard because from time to time they 'borrow' bits for me from other unfortunates when panic sets in. If the stand is constantly on the move, consider a truck or trailer for storage. With an expensive stand, leasing a trailer for a season and racking it out specially can be a wise investment. I will cover storage in more depth later.

■ Budgeting never stops

Once you have completed your budget and had it agreed, surely you can relax. If only! Once you have a budget, you need budgetary control. A good system is your best friend if you can keep on top of it.

■ Flexibility

'Flexibility' is not something I personally approve of. I believe in deciding to do something and sticking to your decision. If you have decided to ignore a particular show, don't let others force you to change your mind. If a new show is launched that you didn't know about, let it test itself in the first year without you.

'Flexibility' is catching. Prevent an epidemic from taking hold.

■ Resist tempting offers . . . mostly!

Make 'resisting tempting offers' an all-year resolution. Even hang it on your wall to remind you. But I bet that good resolution is forgotten as soon as a salesperson rings to tell you that Smiths Circlips has gone into receivership and you can have their space for practically nothing to prevent there being a void in the middle of the show. It's just too tempting to miss. However, don't jump at the chance. The space may turn out to be only a quarter of your costs. Work out the true costs in full. Only when you've done the sums and it still makes sense, go for it.

■ The bargain seeker

One exhibitor I know used to work the other way round. He booked only one show firmly at the beginning of the year, but relied on cancellations and left-over bargains for all the others. He set a finite budget for his exhibiting and, when it was spent, stopped spending for the year. Life was a never-ending panic as he had to keep changing his stand size, sourcing carriers and amending displays, always with about a couple of days to do everything in. Certainly he did get some remarkable bargains, but the strain was hardly worth the effort. Further, I don't believe the adrenaline rush was a good substitute for a disciplined approach and sleeping at nights.

Nevertheless, if you can manage to keep some budget back, you might like to play the game and see how it works for you. Allow enough for a single extra show and hold back until something unmissable comes up. If you never rely on it, you'll probably have some welcome surprises.

■ Target Audiences

Of course, you know who the buyers of your products are, don't you? They might not, however, match the profile of the visitors to the exhibition. In fact, on most occasions only a small proportion of the passing traffic will be interested in buying your products. When you are making your choice of exhibitions to attend, ask to see an analysis of attendees. For a trade show, the organisers will be only too glad to provide you with a breakdown of industry segments represented among the visitors. Work out from this how many would be potential customers of International Spigots. If the proportion is too low, pull out.

■ Study visitor profiles

On the other hand, you may come across trade shows that appear to have no direct relevance to your products at all, but have exactly the right visitor profile. It is a well-known fact that shows promoting capital goods are happy hunting grounds for finance and insurance companies.

All things being equal, go where the audience is right rather than stick with your industry buddies. Companies who have spotted opportunities like that have done extremely well.

■ Look at the quality of the visitor profile

Many show profiles are graded vertically as well as horizontally. They will show the breakdown of visitors into levels of responsibility, decision-making and buying power. A typical breakdown might be: proprietors, directors, managers, administrators, sales staff, students and others. This is just as important as the market segmentation.

One of the advantages of major exhibitions is that they attract senior management and major decision-makers, along with the humble buyers that your salespeople meet on their rounds. Any senior line manager worth their salt will use a trade fair as the prime means of getting an overview of the industry. All new products will be on display. All the other top people will be there too. There will be press receptions, launches and contract signings. A great many rumours start at trade shows and spread like a flu virus in the intense atmosphere.

■ Indirect customers

At every show, however, there will be visitors who, while not actually being potential customers, will benefit from your presence. Intel does not sell microprocessors to the general public. It nevertheless derives benefit from the comfort that PC owners feel when they see an Intel sticker on the side of the machine. So it is worthwhile for Intel to attend computer shows and show the PC-buying public their latest developments.

There will be many people on the periphery of International Spigots' customer base who are interested in what you do. They may be buyers of machines that use your components. So there is always a slightly wider interested audience than you might at first consider.

■ Virgin prospects

Exhibitions are a great place to discover potential customers you didn't realise existed. I remember the case of a contact lens company that decided to promote tinted lenses through stands in shopping malls. At first the company targeted 20 – to 35-year-old women as the most likely buyers. Teenagers were not to be encouraged on the stand as they might put off the target customers. In fact, stand staff soon realised that there was a new buying segment out there that hadn't revealed itself in market research – young women who wanted tinted lenses as an 18th birthday present.

■ Don't rule out anybody by appearance

Many trainers of exhibition staff encourage them to make snap decisions on visitors. They explain how to recognise the real customers and prospects as they approach the stand. Equally they have rules for the early recognition of time-wasters. And all this before a word has been exchanged. This is a very short-sighted attitude. In my experience, you can never be certain until you have spoken to them. You also have to remember that many visitors dress down when going to an exhibition. The CEO who wears a smart suit when you meet him in his office may well wear jeans and a sweater at a trade show, whereas the aspiring clerk in the purchasing department may wear a suit to impress.

■ Sources of industry intelligence

Even those whom many would regard as time-wasters have their uses. I have heard it advocated that visitors who are not from your industry should be courteously turned away. But maybe you shouldn't be so hasty. There is a good reason for at least having a short conversation with those on the periphery of the industry. Market intelligence.

You are unlikely to get accurate information from either your customers or your competitors. But you may from those who have no reason to distort your judgement. Many a good tip has been picked up about an imminent contract or new government initiative from a casual conversation on an exhibition stand, especially if the source derived no benefit from telling you.

■ Student princes

Pity the poor students. They always get a rough deal. Nobody wants to talk to a spotty 19-year-old who is struggling to live on a loan and is wearing Oxfam jeans. How long will it be, everybody asks, until he or she gets access to a corporate chequebook? Often shorter than you think. Ignore or be rude to students at your peril. They have long memories.

On the other hand, be wary of what you tell them. Like many other companies, I have employed students to do research fieldwork for me during their holidays in return for a modest contribution to their clubbing fund. If their questions sound too well-informed, be suspicious.

■ Crumblies

Similarly, don't judge old people on appearance. I have seen them treated abominably. They are patronised by engineers who think they are incapable of understanding the Internet, or anything the least bit technical.

Presumably the stand staff think that the silver-maned old buffer with a stick is a pensioner verging on dementia. If they stopped to think, they might be more careful. What pensioner would travel half-way across the country and shuffle miles round the halls of the NEC when he could be out on the golf course or enjoying the Spanish sun? He does it because he is still involved. Until recently, executives took early retirement at 50 and dropped out. Now many of them have decided that they want to stay in business for the challenge or because their pensions won't support their lifestyles, and have returned to dabble in the crucible. In the main, they are shrewd operators and know every trick in the book.

I remember a very odd character who hobbled up to a stand at IPEX in a suit that must have dated back to the 1950s. He turned out to be a 92-year-old senior director of a family printing company and his brain was alert and decisive. Moreover, he was the man who controlled the budgets for a planned expansion.

■ Scheduling

Scheduling is just as boring as budgeting, isn't it?

Unfortunately, yes, it is. Mind-numbingly so. Nevertheless, scheduling your annual exhibition activity is crucial. Subscribe to one of the excellent guides to the world's exhibitions . . . and dream. You'll find shows in Bali, Vegas and Honolulu.

Realistically, there will be few that are viable propositions. And they will be in mundane places like Birmingham, Dusseldorf and Milan. If your market is a national one, the choice will be even less exotic. In most industries, there will be a flagship international show held annually or biennially, with a couple of major shows strategically placed some time apart, and a number of lower key events either regionally or held for specialist market segments.

■ Is your schedule feasible?

Your first step when you have made your choice is to work out whether it's feasible to attend them all. You need to construct a logistics schedule for the whole year's activities. Make sure there is time to strike at one show, refurbish and be ready to set up at the next. If you can't, you'll have to double your resources.

Allow adequate time for transportation. You might be able to drive to Utrecht in ten hours. That doesn't mean a truck driver will do the same. Although transport may be the stand contractor's responsibility, check that it is booked and that international documentation is put in hand.

■ Individual show scheduling

Once you have your yearly programme settled, surely you can relax, can't you? Well, no. You now need to break it all down into individual events. For each show, you should then produce a detailed production schedule. It should be broken down into areas of responsibility between you, the designers, the contractors and anybody else you intend to hire. If you need help with this, there is a number of proprietary software packages on the market.

■ Make allowances

When scheduling, be realistic and allow for errors, inefficiency and human frailty. As a rule of thumb, things take a third longer to accomplish than you imagine they will. So get into the habit of allowing half as much time again for each task. Then you will be reasonably safe. On the other hand, the exhibition business, especially stand contractors, can perform miracles if pushed. That is, provided two other clients aren't pushing them for miracles at the same time. Try not to call in favours too often.

■ First come, first served

As in so much of industry, size brings power. Great for you if International Spigots is a huge multinational concern able to throw its weight about. Not so good if you happen to be one of the hundreds of medium-sized companies scratching along with the crowd. Then it's first come, first served. So make sure, if you want something, you are first in the queue. This is especially true for exhibition services, like power and telephones. Even then, one of the heavyweights might jump in ahead of you as if you don't exist.

■ Venues – Home and Overseas

Take my advice. Don't exhibit abroad until you've got the hang of it at home. There's a lot to learn and most of it is easier when dealing in your own currency and your own culture. Not only that, when you swear at people, they understand what you mean.

■ Big venues

So let's start with UK venues. At the top of the tree are the monsters, like the National Exhibition Centre near Birmingham. It's a multitude of purpose-built halls, like gigantic airship hangars. Everything there is provided, at a price. If you've forgotten something vital, there is whole back-up industry to call upon within 20 minutes'. It's impersonal but efficient.

There are, however, some disadvantages. At a big show, you'll have to book accommodation early or be prepared to travel long distances. Even though there may be plenty of hotels, they fill up quickly. Hotels also realise that their rooms can command a premium.

■ Holiday towns

Below the big venues is a number of towns that specialise in large exhibition complexes, like Brighton, Bournemouth and Harrogate. They tend to be in 'nice' parts of the country because they saw exhibitions as a way to support holiday hotels out of season. The atmosphere is more pleasant, but you may have other problems like parking, access and technical support. But the accommodation, food and nightlife will be great. A good trade-off in my book.

■ Ordinary places

Then there is a whole spectrum of lesser venues. Almost every town has some place where an exhibition can be held. In many, the function suite in the largest hotel is customarily the host for local events. At these places you have to be self-sufficient.

Many companies do roadshows, on which they tour hotels round the country taking the stand to the customers. A great idea, but make sure you inspect the hotels first, as the dimensions in their banqueting brochures are not always accurate. Broken power sockets take ages to get mended – frequently hotel maintenance men have very rudimentary knowledge of electricity and work office hours only. Even be suspicious of in-house electricians and audio-visual technicians, and preferably take your own.

■ Abroad is full of foreigners

If you must go abroad, you must. We shouldn't be xenophobic. Nevertheless, generally speaking, apart from Australia, the USA and Canada, the further you go from home the more hazardous it becomes, with Russia, Japan and the Philippines providing more than their fair share of horror stories.

If you want to use UK-based suppliers overseas, try to find a stand contractor who is already doing work at the show for somebody else. His transport and crew will be making the trip anyway and the more clients he can accommodate the more he can spread the cost. This is great for some of the big European trade fairs, like Comdex and DRUPA, where a number of UK companies will be exhibiting.

On the other hand, you may feel that you will get better value by using local suppliers. Obviously standards vary round the world, but a reliable contractor over there with an understanding of local customs and an ability to communicate with the organisers counts for a lot. What you may lose in standard of workmanship through local suppliers, you gain in relative freedom from hassle.

■ Accommodation

While you spend the most productive time on the stand, where you stay when off duty is very important.

The easiest solution to accommodating your staff for the duration of the show is to go to the central booking page on the website of a large hotel chain. It's easy. You just tick the boxes – you only need to know how many smokers you have on your staff. Then you give your company credit card number and it's all done. You know in advance that you will have rooms of a given standard and the food will be passable. If something goes wrong, you will be compensated. Peace of mind.

I prefer to do it the hard way. Jump in the car and search for a comfortable private hotel. One that has a roaring log fire in winter and sweeping lawns to enjoy in the summer, and a manager who welcomes you when you arrive and asks if you enjoyed your stay when you leave. The food is prepared individually and the bar stocks the local brew. One reason for choosing this style of accommodation is that once outside the exhibition venue, the last people I want to sit next to at dinner is the crowd from the neighbouring stand.

Big chain hotels are impersonal and I find the constantly circulating stale air gives me a headache in the morning. Call me old-fashioned, but perhaps the high point of staying in a hotel is the freshly cooked breakfast that I never have time for at home.

■ Last-minute Offers

I'll pretend I'm not saying this as it contradicts most of what I have just told you. Especially as the Argonaut would love to hear me admit it. There are opportunities for those of you with a wheeling and dealing mentality. You really can save money by snapping up special offers at the last moment. Every exhibition has its cancellations and void units. And to fill them the organisers would sooner give them away than have a horrible dark hole among other busy stands. The downside is that you have no control over the position or size. Still, you can always say no if you don't like what's on offer.

■ Second stands

Some exhibitors take such units as second stands. It makes sense if you are going to the show anyway and have staff on site. Perhaps you could use such a unit for more down-market products that don't fit in with the image you are trying to create on your smart main stand. A typical case was a sports shoe importer, who used the additional stand to sell factory seconds cheap.

Chapter 3

Booking Exhibitions

'Hello there, have I got a great deal for you!' You vaguely recognise the voice. It's that pushy guy Gary who got your back up from Acme Exhibitions. 'Sorry about the problems you had last year. I'm really going to make it up to you. Promise.'

Last year was something you'd really rather forget, and especially this little runt who was largely responsible. Booking space at exhibitions is worse than buying a new car, choosing curtains and doing your tax return all in one.

The form you have to fill in is seemingly endless and printed in multicoloured sets. And when you've reached the part where you sign, there are still three pages of small print headed 'Terms and Conditions'. It has to be done and the small print has to be read. To be fair to the organisers, most of the terms and conditions are imposed by the venue and cover things like access, build restrictions and charges for things that in the normal world are free. You'll also notice the input of the local health and safety officer.

■ You are the Customer

Exhibition organisers can be heavy-handed at times. I suppose it comes from dealing with some awkward customers. In the main, though, they are fair and helpful if you are reasonable. The main problem I have with them is that they always think they know my business better than I do.

'This is the ideal spot for you.' Gary smirks annoyingly. 'Just what you are looking for.' No, it isn't what you're looking for at all. But they know best. 'Next to the stairs? Of course you can have A43 and A44. But if you take my advice B3 is much better.'

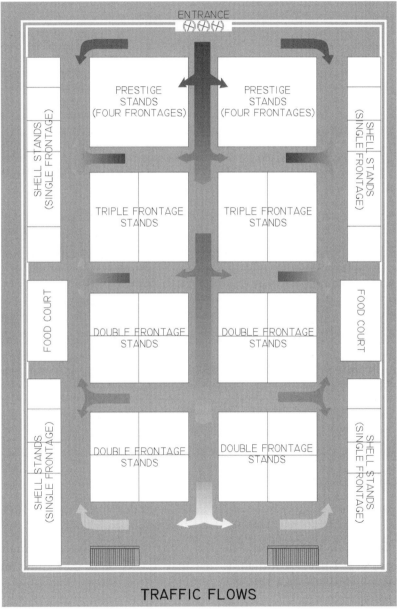

Figure 2 Traffic flows in a typical exhibition hall.

■ Stick to your guns

You are the customer. What Gary and his ilk forget is that you went to the show last year and, during a period when you weren't on duty, you took the trouble to study the traffic flow. On the face of it B3 would seem to be the better site, but it faces away from the general flow. Whereas A43, a smaller site, is at one of the busiest spots in the show. Combine it with its neighbour, A44, and it be almost as big as B3. See Figure 2 for a typical traffic flow.

■ Negotiate creatively

What you should also remember is that, while the prestigious island site near the entrance may be expensive, an equivalent space might be booked in a less fashionable part of the hall by combining a block of four small spaces. When the spaces are booked individually, the price saving probably would not be great, if any. By taking a block, you might be able to negotiate a hefty discount because it saves the salesperson work. Their call to you for a small stand takes just as long as for a large one, but their commission is much less.

Organisers are often open to negotiation. You should get a discount if you book two spaces. As time goes on and there are still large gaps, the organisers may start to lose their nerve and allow you to trade up to a better site for a small increase in price. Why not give the salesperson a call from time to time? That's if the annoying Gary doesn't pester you first.

■ The Site Plan and Traffic Flows

If you haven't been to that particular exhibition before, study the site plan. Try to visualise it in 3D. Imagine you are a visitor coming in. You've just registered and received your guidebook. You are completely disoriented. Which way would you go first?

■ Patterns of movement

Some people work to a system, starting at one corner and following the aisles back and forth in sequence. They aim to see it all.

Others, the ones beloved by show organisers, dive in without any plan and head straight down the middle. If they go down the main aisle, the chances are they'll come back along the next on one side or the other. So, in theory, stands in the aisles either side of the centre aisle should be facing the other way. Theory doesn't always work, because the traffic becomes fragmented as visitors stop to look at stands, then head off in new directions. What we can say is that traffic tends to be heaviest near the centre and around any special attractions.

■ Corners and galleries

The corners and gallery attract the least traffic. Prices of space there generally reflect the footfall in the aisles, but not always. This is because organisers might for convenience put all spaces in one block at one price. So study the plan carefully. There are bargains to be had for those who do their homework.

■ Special attractions

Being next to a special attraction sometimes attracts a premium. This isn't always justified. While crowds might gather next to the dry ski slope, they will be watching the action and not looking at your stand. They block the space and prevent visitors getting a full view of your stand. Also, they will be mentally switched to entertainment rather than business mode.

From an aesthetics point of view, attractions can be less appealing. Articles like parachute drops and climbing walls will dwarf nearby stands, making them appear less imposing than they would be elsewhere. Also special attractions normally involve noise, and that can be really distracting.

■ Love Thy Neighbour

You can frequently persuade the organiser's salesperson to mark your site plan up for you so that you know companies which have booked spaces round the one that interests you. Gary will be only too pleased to gloat over how much cash he is lifting from your rivals.

■ Segmented layouts

Organisers like to compartmentalise their exhibitions, putting all companies of one type in one area. Lubricant manufacturers, motor homes, lawn mowers. Lump them all together. Of course, there are advantages to all from this policy. Buyers can compare products, like with like. However, try to keep some distance between you and direct competitors, even if you get on well with them. You don't want them to know who you are deep in discussion with. That is unless you are selling on price and you are much cheaper.

■ ASBOs

Over time, you also get to know which neighbours are less than neighbourly. Some love loud and spectacular presentations interspersed with blaring music. The noise irritates more and more as the show progresses, but the worst aspect is the overflow of spectators they attract who blank off part of your stand for 15 minutes every hour. Of course, if you are one of these extrovert exhibitors, you wonder what all the fuss is about. It's tough luck for these miserable killjoys who want to spoil your fun. You wouldn't complain if they did it. Not half you wouldn't!

■ Settling disputes

From experience, I believe that disputes between stand-holders are best settled face to face if possible. There is usually a workable and amicable compromise. Complaints to the organisers rarely settle anything, partly because they don't want to upset clients who might come again next year, and partly because the rights and wrongs of the case get lost in industry politics.

■ The Visible and (Hidden) Extras

Decide early on which venue services you really must have. They are always ridiculously expensive. Here are a few points to discuss with the rep. I mention them here in passing, but will be covering them fully later.

■ Must haves

Electricity is a must, and it is always best to bite the bullet and err on the generous side. Have at least one more socket than you think you will need. Plumbing is something you can usually do without, unless you are cooking on the stand. Telephone lines are a must if you need access to the Internet, although there are now ways round this. Otherwise, have a dedicated mobile phone for the stand staff. This has the additional advantage that it can be taken away and used after opening hours.

■ Security

Security is a difficult area. Once again, it's expensive but on balance worth the money. In developing countries always, but always, pay for the man with the military cap and big moustache. If you don't, things will disappear.

■ Cleaning

Some venues offer cleaning services. If you are tidy and careful, why should you need them? They knock out your connections and move furniture around. If you have carpets and furniture that attract fluff and those bits of polystyrene from your packing materials that cling to everything, take a portable vacuum cleaner. Always have a cleaning roster for staff.

Chapter 4

Planning the Stand

■ Creativity vs Practicality

Now for the exciting bit. What are you going to do on the rectangle of exhibition hall floor or in that shell scheme cave? It's a blank canvas.

■ The student's idealistic view

I often visit art colleges on their open days to see what new talent is on the market. Too often I am disappointed. When briefs are given to students to design exhibition stands, they are issued in sweeping generalisations, possibly mentioning brand values, product strategies and target markets. I have little complaint with that, as far as it goes.

Little is mentioned, however, of all the things that the average client insists on including or the constraints imposed by the venue. So the students let the creative juices flow in abundance and produce great works of almost sculptural quality. Wonderful shapes abound, structures tower into the rafters and amazing new materials are devised. After countless sleepless nights waiting for inspiration and months of careful crafting, the design is submitted. Marks are awarded on the basis of originality and creative flair.

■ Planet reality

Unfortunately, in the real world, it is never like that. Practicality rules and creativity comes second. An exhibition stand is above all a workplace. Like all workplaces, it must include certain basic elements to enable the staff to perform their task efficiently. The venue will impose constraints too, in terms of height, types of material, access and floor loading. And common sense dictates that certain designs work, while others don't. Common sense is not on the art college's curriculum.

Use height wherever available. Property management company stand showing impact on small site

■ Don't forget the visitors

One of the biggest mistakes many students make is that they allow insufficient provision for the most important things on a stand – the visitors. There must be at least standing space for them to talk to staff, view graphic panels and examine products. If they are expected to discuss confidential business, there will have to be comfortable seating in an enclosed area. Not only must there be room on the stand to learn and be entertained, but visitors must be able to enter and leave easily.

Neither is this lack of consideration restricted to students. Many experienced stand designers seem to forget that an exhibition exists for the benefit of the visitors as well as exhibitors. Obvious, isn't it? You would have thought so.

But look around critically at the next exhibition you visit. Much of it will give you the impression that you and your fellow visitors are not welcome. There are barriers, both physical and psychological, between you and what you want to learn from many of the stands you visit. Make an assessment of which stands work and which don't. And then ask yourself why.

■ It's Your Shop Window

Remember what I said about the similarity between exhibiting and retailing?

If you are selling business to business, your stand is the nearest thing you have to a shop. It is often the only opportunity that many of your customers have for personal contact with your organisation. If they are on your sales force's calling schedule, customers will meet a salesperson a couple of times a year. They might be treated to the latest company video or flipped through a PowerPoint presentation. What they rarely get is the benefit of technical advice from a sales engineer, a chat about bigger discounts with the sales director or a view of the full range of products displayed properly and possibly working. All of these can happen on your stand.

■ First impressions

It's an old adage that you never get a second chance to make a first impression. Impressions in business are made in several ways. The most potent, we are told, are made aurally, through the telephone, and visually, by the things we see most often – advertising, sponsorship, truck liveries and exhibition stands.

■ Your company in a box

Of the visual means, exhibition stands leave the deepest impression. At an exhibition, outsiders see all that your company has to offer encapsulated in a box. Its branding, its people, its philosophy, its products. Even its friendliness and willingness to serve. Nowhere else can a customer or prospect get all that in one hit. Even a visit to your factory won't achieve that.

■ Making the Best of Your Site

Having examined at some length the choice of site, let's assume that you've bitten the bullet and now the space is booked.

In an ideal world, every site is an island site, allowing your stand to be seen and entered from every side. Reality dictates that most sites have a maximum of two sides visible and open.

■ The island site

Wouldn't it be wonderful if you were one of the lucky few, and that superb prime island site in full view of the entrance to the exhibition hall was yours to do with as you will. That would be the nearest you would ever get to the student's blank canvas. What an opportunity!

Yet what normally happens? This space is inevitably taken by the industry leader, who uses it to thrust on everybody their position of power and dominance. The stand will be highly corporate and expensive looking, but without an ounce of imagination, humour or humanity. The smartly suited staff are remote and offhand. The counter, if there is one, inaccessible. This is about making a statement, and often it's an unpleasant statement. We're the tough guys, and you'd better remember who's at the top when you tour the show among the lesser mortals!

■ If only . . .

A plea from the heart. If you take one of these prime sites, please try to set the tone for the whole exhibition. The site offers you untold opportunities for visual stimulation, for exciting experiences and involvement. An island site allows the most access you can have. Exploit that. Let the creative juices flow like Niagara. Let the office juniors at the design consultancy have their say. Head each concept board with the word 'fun'. And give every member of the stand staff smiley face badges.

Planning for the best positioning of equipment can be complex.
A second storey takes the pressure off ground space

Don't partition off a huge portion of that prime site for a hospitality area. If you must have an enclosed area for discussion, why not take another stand elsewhere or book a separate room at the venue? Better still, have a second deck, and put it up there. Usually, sites in the centre of the hall can extend to quite a height and this facility allows exciting visual possibilities. The glory of an island site is to see visitors wandering all over it, going in all directions, trying things out and enjoying every part of it.

■ Down to earth

OK, stop dreaming. Island sites are not for most of us. The greater proportion must slum it in the body of the hall with the industry hoi polloi. That's not to say that we must be content with second best. What it means is that the options are fewer, so you have to be even more imaginative.

■ Focus your stand

First, make your position work for you, not against you. Focus your stand like a spotlight into the main traffic flow. Put your strongest, most blatant features where the most visitors will see them. Angle the stand entrance towards the traffic flow, if there is one, so that it feels natural for passing visitors to step aboard. Use plasma screens and monitors to entice the curious.

If you have an auditorium area, position it so that during a presentation passing visitors can see over the heads of the audience. They will pause and see what's on offer, and perhaps come back for the next performance. Of course, you should also consider the perverse individuals who approach from the wrong direction. That would be me.

■ The friendly end

The shell scheme exhibitors needn't feel out of it, either. If there's one endearing fact about these small stands it is that they are not intimidating. How can they be, when the visitor is at most three feet from a company managing director in his shirt sleeves putting lollipops into a jar? If you have 20 square metres or less, don't try and stand on your dignity. You haven't any. So make everything fun. You will probably have just the front open, so there has to be a real incentive for passers-by to enter the stand. You could treat it like a stall in an oriental bazaar and stock it to the ceiling with products, then stand in the front hawking your wares. Anything that creates a feeling of drama.

■ A sense of theatre

Speaking of drama, perhaps you have noticed how like a small theatre your shell stand is. You have a proscenium arch, focusing attention inwards towards your little stage. Behind, you have a backdrop, which sets the scene. You and your staff are the cast, performing on demand every time a prospect enquires what you do or have to offer.

■ Projection

Stretching the imagination a little bit? Perhaps so, but there is one theatrical technique you should attempt – projection. Actors project themselves into the auditorium. Your auditorium is the aisle in front of your stand. Although you don't own it and have no right to occupy it, there is nothing to stop you projecting your aura over it. It's a rare phenomenon to be irresistibly drawn to a stand as if by some mystic force, but it sometimes happens. There's really no magic. It's just that the stand staff are happy and want to spread their happiness. They have a good story to tell and enjoy telling it. And they want your business so much that they are willing you to talk to them.

■ New Build or System

When considering the techniques for building a stand-alone structure (and possibly elements within a shell scheme), you have a choice of building from scratch or using a modular system. There is a cost premium on the purpose-built stand, but possibly not as much as you would expect. Also bear in mind that in both cases you are only hiring the stand, unless you stipulate from the start that you want to buy it. It's a sobering thought that, although you may have been able to buy a small house for the price you have paid, the structure is yours only during the show.

■ Custom-built stands

Some of the advantages of each are obvious. If you build from scratch, you can have exactly what you want. It can be in any approved material and be as off-the-wall in design as you are prepared to go. For the company doing one big show a year, it can probably be justified. More than one show, and you start to hit snags. Rarely can you book identical spaces at different shows, so you have to compromise with a structure that breaks into units that can be moved separately. Then there are the problems of keeping it immaculate between shows and touching up the inevitable scratches and nicks.

■ Modular systems

Modular systems are designed to be . . . well, modular. Each system contains a large set of components that fit together and can be made to fill any space. There tends to be a certain sameness about the finished result, although that may be something that we in the industry notice more than exhibition visitors. Many of today's systems look professional, being made from space-age aluminium extrusions or lattice.

■ A vast range to choose from

In my view some of the older systems are a little impersonal and cold, but these are being augmented by some really attractive designs. The manufacturers are continually trying to make them more flexible, so that more adventurous constructions will be possible. Just like kitchen units, there is a vast array of qualities to choose from, ranging from cheap and tacky to vastly expensive that from the cost should have been fashioned by Tiffany from platinum and precious stones. Some of the nicest and most versatile aluminium systems are made in Germany.

Systems mainly comprise a framework of aluminium extrusions into which are slotted rectangular panels. The panels can be in whatever material you choose: felt-covered boards, graphics, mirrors, transparent sheet or back-lit panels. The extrusions vary greatly in complexity. Systems like Octanorm are octagonal in cross-section, which allows you to depart from the boxy look. Modul and other German systems use sections and curved panels that can be used to make round pillars and even round seating areas.

For most systems full catalogues of components are published by the manufacturer. The sizes and strengths are known and often Computer Aided Design (CAD) databases are available for designers. So the designer can work within a system and be able to predict the properties of a structure. The manufacturers are pleased to help out if the calculations get too complex or need to be checked.

Modular systems needn't lack imagination (photo courtesy of Nomadic Display)

■ Hire first, buy later

Companies who do a great deal of exhibiting might start by hiring from system suppliers and then buy a kit of components from the manufacturer. They can then use it just how and when they want, in the knowledge that if they need any more parts these can be hired and will fit. The stand designer can maintain a database of the client's components on the CAD system and know instantly how much extra will be required for a one-off.

■ What You Need – Wish-List

When you first start to plan your stand, there's so much to think of and so many people to consider. You must manage the company's needs and resources. So why not hold a brainstorming session with everybody involved? Find out what everyone wants to achieve from the stand and their possible input. Getting them involved at an early stage encourages them to 'own' the project.

■ Input fosters commitment

That first meeting is often surreal. Half your invitees don't turn up because they can't think more than three months ahead. The ones who do will argue about insignificant matters that can be sorted out at a later date. Colour schemes, demonstrations and availability of new products seem to be favourite bones of contention. Don't discourage them, because their enthusiasm will be useful later. Note their opinions and move on to more pressing matters. If you can agree a schedule of shows, stand sizes, production programme and responsibilities, you have made great progress.

■ Allocating budgets

Larger corporate stands often act as an umbrella to cover a number of product groups, each with their own clearly defined section. In such cases, it is important to sort out at a very early stage how much space will be allowed for each product manager. A convenient means of budgeting is to rent the space out to them in square metres; however, this is often less than fair as some products will have bigger footprints than others and may require more space to demonstrate. A fairer way to allocate budget is through anticipated turnover that will be derived from exhibiting. A more radical approach is to get them to tender for space. Those with the greatest commitment then get the best space.

■ Wish-lists

At this initial planning stage, ask everybody for their wish-list of features and components. Here are some of the most frequently requested items:

- Reception counter and stools.
- Video/DVD player and monitors/plasma screens/projector.
- Workstations running simulations or on-line.
- Enclosed hospitality/discussion area.
- Chat area, with comfy chairs or sofa and coffee table.
- Store cupboard for literature, samples, food and drink and coats.
- Display boards and graphics.

- Presentation theatre with benches or bum-bars.
- Literature racks.
- Product plinths.
- Bar and catering facilities, with stools, chairs etc.
- Water dispenser or coffee machine.

There are many more. When all the requests are in, you will find that if all the inanimate objects are included, there will be no room for human beings. But it is better to list and prioritise them now than forget something vital and have to squeeze it in later. If there just isn't room for something, stand your ground now.

Components can vary in size and importance, so you should decide on how big or impressive you want them to be. A useful way of categorising them is by giving items that sell products an A status, items that make the stand attractive to visitors a B status and items that are purely administrative or for comfort a C status.

■ How Many People Will Be on the Stand?

Before you can tie down the physical elements of the stand, work out how many people will be occupying it, both staff and anticipated visitors. Each person should be allowed one square metre, in order to stand or sit on an upright chair. Two people in conversation normally face each other about 60 cm apart, which is about handshaking distance. When meeting, you approach each other head on, and when parting one party turns to one side or the other. So you can see that allowing space for just standing is insufficient.

One approach is to draw out the stand on squared paper, then use cut-out people to scale in plan view. For each person, draw a circle to represent their personal space. Move them around to get a good idea of how much room they will occupy.

■ The person in charge

On every stand, there should always be a senior staff member present to receive VIPs and make decisions beyond the capability of the sales staff. This senior person might be the stand manager (more about their responsibilities later), but, if not, should acknowledge the stand manager's overall responsibilities.

■ Sales people

How many salespeople should you take off the road and put on the stand? It's an age-old question. As a rough guide, try a ratio of about one salesperson to every three visitors expected on the stand at any time. Whether or not this will be the right proportion depends on the type of exhibition and will only be learnt through experience. Generally speaking, if you have too many staff hovering ready to pounce, visitors are intimidated. If you have too few, frustration will result and you might miss a valuable buyer.

■ Demonstrators

While the sales staff take precedence, other people may have to be present. If you are demonstrating some complex piece of machinery, you may need a demonstrator or engineer present to operate, open the inspection ports and remove parts for examination. If you are doing a cookery demonstration, you'll need chefs and, equally important, washer-uppers.

■ Receptionists

Most stands have some type of reception counter. If the receptionist is merely registering visitors and answering queries, one person is probably adequate, with a reserve to take over during lunch and breaks. If you have something more complicated in mind, have two receptionists.

■ Transport

Getting the stand to the venue is normally the responsibility of the stand builder. He will calculate just how much vehicle space all the parts will take up, and while he may be happy to take your literature and samples to the show as well, don't count on it. When the time comes, there may not be space. If you are going abroad, of course, it's in everybody's interests to make the most effective use of transport, so warn the builder in good time so that a large enough truck can be booked. Think also of his employees. Print is heavy and his craftspeople are not paid to do your back-breaking work for you. They have enough of their own.

You will need to get your personnel to the venue and to move them to and from their hotels. A minibus is an ideal runabout for your staff and can be used to collect invited overseas visitors from airports.

■ Getting Consensus

That's the initial meeting taken care of. Get as much agreement as you can from your colleagues. Tie them down to action points and delivery dates. Get them to commit to everything being supplied or organised by their departments. Then publish:

- Full minutes of the meeting.
- A full production schedule.

After giving them a couple of days to digest these, you will need to contact the recipients to check that they understand.

Chapter 5

Choosing a Designer and Stand Contractor

Designing and building exhibition stands is not for amateurs. Believe me, I do it. And I redo it for a lot of people who think they'd like to try. Even some professionals don't get it right. So where do you look for help?

■ Where to Look

■ Using your agency

Many companies approach their advertising agency, PR company or sales promotion agency. There is much to be said for involving them. The design of the stand will be kept 'on brand'. It will follow the style of existing campaigns. Also, you will probably be allocated a junior account executive who will take a lot of the administrative burden off your shoulders. And, of course, like most of your other marketing activities, there will be somebody to share the blame if something goes awry.

The downside is a small matter of commission. You may be lucky and get away with their standard rate – 17.65 per cent normally. More likely it will be 30–45 per cent on bought-in services. And that nice young account executive won't be cheap either, charged out by the hour, the mile and the meal, and all justified on the job card. Also be aware that the account executive may have little more experience of exhibitions than you do. Nevertheless, if you have any doubts about your ability to handle pressure and frustration, I would advise taking this less stressful (for you, that is) route. Of course, the agency doesn't actually employ the designer. They buy-in their services just as you could.

■ The direct approach

So why not cut out the middleman? He who dares, saves. There are several routes. You could approach a designer or specialist design agency and let them select a contractor of their choice. In doing so, make certain the designer is an experienced stand designer. Many a graphic designer will be happy to take a break from Quark and Illustrator to have a go at something more challenging. Insist on the real thing and ask to see the portfolio.

The advantage is that professional designers and builders work together and will be on the same wavelength. They will probably use the same CAD software, very useful when tweaks are needed and time is running short. A good designer will design something unique to you that meets your brief exactly.

■ The stand contractor

Alternatively, you could go directly to the contractor, who will either use their own in-house designer or bring in a freelancer. This option will probably result in a more practical but less creative approach. Stand builders are only human and like to stay within their comfort zones. They will also try and recycle what they have in store, given half a chance. When you are given the grand tour of the industrial unit in Acton, take note of what's lying about. Some of it will probably appear in your stand. Nothing wrong with that, provided it hasn't stilted the design concept or you are asked to pay full price for second-hand parts.

■ Ask the organisers

There's a lot to be said for asking the exhibition organisers for their advice. The designers and contractors they recommend will be familiar with the show and venue. They won't risk suggesting a cowboy outfit that will cause them problems or let down the appearance of their show. Often the contractor they suggest will be the one constructing their shell scheme. If so, it might save you money and it is likely that workers and technicians from the company will be resident on site all through the show.

■ Directories

Then there are directories and Yellow Pages. Pages and pages of names to choose from there. If I were seeking a designer I would tend to go for the ones who don't spend too much money on advertising, but that's a personal preference. All things being equal, choose people who are near at hand. Exhibiting requires much closer liaison with suppliers than other marketing activities. It's great to be able to nip down the road and resolve a problem or check a swatch in half an hour.

■ Shortlisting

Most companies initially approach several designers or builders. All should be visited if only to satisfy yourself on the quality of their craftsmanship. If you can, go to a show where one of their stands can be seen. Look through their portfolios. Every designer has a style, and the chances are that whatever your brief asks for, that style will show through. So pick one with a style that pleases you, and for heaven's sake don't pick one that grates on you. It doesn't matter if you agree on everything else, if you have different tastes it will never work. Divergences between client and designer over style issues become irreconcilable over time.

Relationships between client and designer can become very close. A new designer has to learn much about your company in a short time. Stand designers often become almost part of the staff, with encyclopaedic knowledge of the product range, corporate ID and senior management likes and dislikes. They are in the main very loyal and will defend their clients stoutly against outside criticism.

■ What to look out for in the workshop

If you are looking round builders' premises, watch out for certain things. How good is their production planning? If you see a job going through, you should be able to detect the progress through the shop, with elements being built, stacked and packaged as a smooth process.

Do they have their own transport? Often they will hire vehicles in from outside for specific jobs, but it's handy to know that there's a truck back at base to bring up that forgotten plinth.

Are the workforce friendly? If you've had to work with a team with the threat of redundancy hanging over them, you'll know how unpleasant it can be. And the fault isn't yours. Try to hit it off with the chippies and fabricators, as you'll probably be asking them to perform beyond the call of duty. Most are the salt of the earth.

General tidiness – or lack of it – is something you'll notice when walking round. However, be prepared to accept that stand building isn't a normal production process. Sometimes the lads will have been up all night to meet a tight deadline, and sweeping up shavings will be low on the list of priorities.

Often there is one designer or contractor you hit it off with straight away. If that is so, don't waste the time of the others by asking them to pitch, even if your company has a policy of competitive tendering.

■ Competitive pitching

If you want to have a choice of approaches, shortlist three at most. You don't get better results by asking more to pitch. Often it is the reverse. Everybody, except the really hungry (and less demanded) designers, puts in effort in inverse relation to the size of the pitch list. Really busy designers, by definition the most popular, may decline to take part.

One approach, gaining in popularity, is to choose one designer from the outset and ask for several concepts. Here the designer knows they have the job and so is motivated. They will do their utmost to produce original and very different designs. However, be prepared to pay for them.

■ The Brief

In your design brief, you should try to convey the impression you want the design to have on visitors. If International Spigots is an established company, anxious to impress everybody with their reliability and stability in a volatile industry, ask for something solid and conservative. If your stand resembles an unassailable fortress, that is how International Spigots will be viewed.

On the other hand, if you want to be regarded as mavericks, striking out on your own with original ideas, brief the designer to give you something radical and challenging to the eye. Whichever approach you decide to take, the International Spigots stand should have that indefinable something that makes passers-by stop and stare. The so-called 'wow-factor.'

The following are some guidelines on writing and delivering briefs.

■ Written brief

Always issue a written brief and have a full briefing meeting for each contender. Don't be tempted to brief them all in one session. Nobody asks searching questions at the session and you will be hounded for days to come by telephone calls.

■ Creative freedom

While you should set out all the necessary requisites and constraints, try not to be too constrictive. Allow the designer some room to be creative.

■ Background information

Give the design team as much background material as you can on the company, to help them understand the corporate culture, marketing strategy and your market position. A pack containing the annual report, a selection of brochures and pulls of current ads would be ideal. If you can spare the time, take the team round the factory and showroom. They need to breathe in the International Spigots' air and absorb the International Spigots' dust through their pores.

▪ Objectives

Most important of all, state your objectives and keep them simple. The designer must know what you want to achieve.

▪ Wish-list and constraints

Outline your wish-list and constraints. You don't need to go through the show handbook. The designer will do that as a matter of course. The exception to this is if you want to bend the rules – you might, for instance, have agreed with the organisers to exceed the maximum height.

▪ Budget

Not only should you quote the budget, you should also stipulate what it includes and excludes. And if necessary ask for a breakdown. It may be that you are funding the stand from two or more budgets.

▪ Who pays?

On a competitive pitch, should you pay for the contenders' speculative work? A few companies do, but most don't. Even those that do pay barely enough to cover expenses, let alone time and bought-in services. For design agencies, pitching is an expensive fact of life. They grumble endlessly about it, but accept that there will always be somebody prepared to pitch for nothing. However, as clients, you should be aware that there is no such thing as a free lunch and that you and others have to fund this endless round of speculative pitching.

■ Making the Choice

■ All on the same day

Try to get all the designers to present to you on the same day. This makes it as fair as possible. Some will do anything to be the last to pitch because they feel that that will make them more memorable. They may ask if they can come the next day. If you feel that any are trying this tactic and can't make it on the day chosen, see them before rather than after the others.

■ Presentation styles

Styles of presentation vary considerably. A design studio may send down a team of 'suits', trained at public speaking, with a studio-produced PowerPoint laptop presentation and a beautifully crafted model. It's very slick and persuasive. The next person through the door might be a young fellow with piercings and jeans. He will open a pad on the table and self-consciously show you his sketches.

It's difficult not be influenced by the style of presentation, but you must try. The sophisticated presentation skills of the former team don't necessarily mean their design is more professional or that they will be better organised. Neither necessarily will the drop-out be more creative or cheaper. Try not to make snap decisions. Leave models and visuals in the boardroom and revisit them tomorrow with a fresh mind. Bring in others to have a look and comment.

You should choose on the potential of the contenders, not the finished product. It is often a matter of luck whether or not a designer gets it right first time. Look beyond the design you are presented with to imagine what it could become.

■ Swift decision

Don't delay your decision. Make it swift and decisive. Confirm in writing or by email. Then stick to your decision.

■ Debriefing

Debrief all the contenders, including the losers. They have put in a lot of work and it's only fair to give an appraisal of their efforts. If their ideas are too pedestrian, tell them honestly. They won't improve unless you do. If they were too expensive, they'll hopefully come up with something cheaper next time.

■ If you're not satisfied

If none of the designs is right, you can bring in new contenders, but I believe in allowing the best of the first group another chance, unless they clearly aren't up to the job. They've tried hard and earned the right to have another go.

Sometimes you might see elements of one design that you like and parts of another. How do you resolve that? The honourable way is to approach one of the parties and see if a cash settlement can be agreed for part of the design. If this is not accepted, copyright dictates that you can't use it. Normally, a sense of survival overcomes the designer's wounded pride. It is an unfortunate fact of life that clients do pinch their ideas and use them seemingly without any qualms. They do so in the knowledge that no designer is in a position to take a large company to court as only token damages are likely.

■ Over budget

Another problem is the contender who presents a great design, but is way over budget. Even if you have the funds, you should not rise to this. It's a try-on and the designer has not met the terms of the brief. Strictly speaking, the designer should be rejected or given the option to prepare another design within the given budget. In practice, it all ends in horse-trading. The correct way to present a project over budget is to propose a basic design that meets the cost constraint, then present the extras as optional ex-budget items, the so-called shopping list approach.

■ Terms of Engagement and Contracts

When you've made your choice of designer or builder, accept them formally as suppliers, subject to contract. The contract will probably arrive within a few days as everybody will want to get into production as soon as possible. The contract will give the stand specification in detail. Study it carefully and check that nothing has been conveniently omitted.

■ Keep one or two reserves

If your first choice doesn't cut the mustard, you may have to revert to your second choice. I have known busy contractors, who hate to turn down a job, accept a project they can only complete by subcontracting. The subcontractors, taking the brief second-hand, produce a unsatisfactory construction, and the result is that the job is be taken away from the original contractor. Unfortunately this situation is more common than it should be. One idea is to stipulate in your contract that you want to know the names of all subcontractors and see examples of their work too.

■ The contract

The contract on a reasonably sized stand will be a fixed price contract, with possibly three equal staged payments. The first will be due on commissioning – that's now. The second will be when construction is complete, prior to going on site, and the third either when it has first been erected, or at the end of the exhibition, when it has been struck. Of course, you can agree to any terms you like. On a smaller stand, you might agree on just two payments. The concept behind staged payments is to enable the builder to purchase the raw materials at the beginning of the project, to pay his wages half-way through and keep the last chunk as his profit.

■ Project changes

The exhibition business being what it is, changes take place between the signing of the contract and completion. How are these handled? Normally through a device called a 'Project Change Notice', or something similar. This is a docket on which the amendment to the original specification is written, with its associated cost. Work cannot proceed on the change until an authorised representative of the client has signed it.

■ Project plan

On a complex project, a client may insist on project plan with sign-off dates. If work on a stage is not completed by its appropriate sign-off, there will be a penalty or delay on the next staged payment.

Chapter 6

Into Production

With the contract signed, production can proceed in earnest. Early in the project, you'll probably be seeing a lot of the designer and the builder, but this tends to ease off. I would advocate allowing a good three days at the start to go through all the detail, look at swatches and finishes, and agree on the technical matters.

■ Plans, Models and Visuals

In all probability, initial models and visuals will have been presented to you at the pitch stage. They are usually a good starting point for discussion, and will be altered many times. Until recently, the traditional way to present concepts was in the form of models.

■ Models

Solid models made from foamboard are disappearing fast. Although they are very tactile, they are inconvenient and difficult to change. I even remember one being crushed by lift doors on the way to a pitch. Perhaps the worst factor was that they gave you an unrealistic idea of how the stand would look on site, since you tended to look down on it with a three-quarter view, like some Greek god.

■ Hand-drawn visuals

Or you might get a set of artistic watercolour or magic marker visuals. They are normally small works of art, just like architects' renderings. Great skill has gone into making everything as dramatic as possible. Shiny surfaces gleam. Spotlights cast brilliant beams. Visitors are engrossed in conversation. But we all know in our hearts that the stand will never look like that. Unfortunately they are seldom to scale, with all the practical connotations that go with 'artist's impressions'.

■ Computer modelling

This is where designing on a computer comes into its own, perhaps working initially in a CAD package and transferring the computer model to a 3D modelling and rendering package. I prefer working the other way round, modelling in 3D from the start and using realistic viewpoints. The visuals attained can be very lifelike, especially when people have been added. You also know that the scale is correct and that if something is shown on the visual to fit into a space, it will indeed fit that space on the day.

Building the stand in 3D on the computer is a great way to learn about its characteristics, since it is the nearest you get to building without wielding a saw and screwdriver. Each electronic piece has to be made exactly to size. If they don't meet, the computer allows you to enlarge them so they do. Then the designer can lay off the dimensions for the real component. Then when everything is just as everybody likes it, the CAD software can plot the plans.

There is also the benefit that computer files can be whizzed around the world. If you want to design in London and take advantage of local construction rates for a fair in Hong Kong, there is no problem. AutoCAD is used there as well.

■ Designing systems on computer

Designing modular system stands using a computer is much easier than on a drawing board. Many system manufacturers issue CAD databases of all their components which can be used to construct a 3D model. When it is approved by management, a list of parts with hire or purchase prices can be output at the end. When working with complicated trusses and lattice work, this is much easier than any other method. And you know at the end that it will work.

Sometimes a company will keep a stock of modular parts they have already bought. The exhibition manager wants to know what can be accomplished with what they own and how much they might have to hire in. The designer will import the database of existing parts and shuffle it round to make a stand to fit an exhibition space. If there aren't enough components, the gaps are then easily identified and filled from hire stock.

Computers have revolutionised stand design. Unfortunately, they don't give us any more time, as now people expect everything done more quickly. The one thing I draw the line at is geodesic domes. I've never yet got one to work properly in CAD.

■ Textures and finishes

Another advantage of 3D modelling is that textures, finishes and even the graphics on the panels can be simulated under different lighting conditions. Aluminium and stainless steel look great on properly lit models. If possible get the modeller to 'ray-trace' the visual. This means that the computer simulates all the shadows and reflections from each light source. It can take some time but the results are worth it.

■ Views

It is also relatively easy to do several views of a stand. I favour, visitor points of view (VPOVs), which simulate exactly what a visitor sees when approaching down an aisle. These are great for assessing sightlines and gauging the impact of visual elements.

■ Walkthroughs

Some clients will request 'walkthroughs'. These are short movies of what a visitor would theoretically see as they approach and walk through the stand. Sounds great, doesn't it? Almost like a fly-on-the-wall documentary, in fact. In practice, I discourage them for two reasons. The first is the huge amount of rendering time to do the job properly. This expends computer time and budget that could better be used elsewhere. The second is that it never gives a satisfactory simulation of how we as humans view the world about us.

The walkthrough employs a virtual camera that tracks its way through the virtual stand, looking dead ahead or at a given angle. Humans don't behave that way. We look about us constantly, glancing at a graphic panel, stopping to be greeted by a salesperson, bending down to examine a product on a plinth. Of course, we can get the virtual camera to do all that, but the conventions of cinematography, which our eyes have come to accept, don't allow for all this meandering about. I could go on. Anyway, take my word for it. 'Walkabouts' are bad news.

■ Changes to the model

Making changes to a computer model is obviously easier than to a foamboard model or hand-drawn visuals. Yet it isn't quite as simple as many clients think. What might seem to be an easy change when asked for verbally might have considerable spatial implications to the stand.

'It's only a tiny alteration. I'd like the cupboard a couple of feet longer. Can you amend the visuals, so I can see what it looks like? Not a problem, is it?' Well, yes it is, but it's usually simpler to do the job than explain everything else that has to be rejigged. The model has to be amended and then rendered. Probably three or four hours' work. On one quite small stand I had to undertake 13 redesigns and sets of visuals. One of them was when the client requested switching from square columns to round. Apparently he couldn't imagine it with a small change to the columns.

■ Production Schedule

Nobody's favourite job, but it has to be done. If you are into critical path analysis, here's an excellent chance to practise your skills.

Jot down the key dates. These might be:

- Commissioning date – initial payment due.
- Book hotels, flights and other logistics.
- Brief stand designer.

- Brief production director for stand exhibits.
- Order ex-stock items.
- Order specially prepared exhibits (e.g. cutaways).
- Brief script writer for product demo.
- Design meeting for client, designer and builder to finalise stand design details.
- Approve and sign off design and budgets.
- Brief contractor with designer.
- View carpet swatches, paints and finishes.
- Agree and hire furniture.
- Agree electronics and hire equipment requirement.
- Brief graphics designer for display panels.
- Approve script for product demo.
- Approve display panels.
- Stand staff training day.
- Trial build at contractor's premises.
- Inspect and test exhibits.
- Ship stand and collateral.
- Rehearsal for product demonstration.
- Second stage payment due.
- Show build starts.
- Tech rehearsal.
- Show opens.
- Show closes.
- Third stage payment due.
- Show strike complete.
- Reconciliation and debriefing.

Work backwards from the day the venue doors open. Estimate how long each task will take and double it, on the principle that jobs always take at least a third longer to complete than anybody estimates. If possible, add in a week just before shipping the stand, to allow for contingency.

Of course, many activities run concurrently, so your plan will have several threads. It's useful if all the threads are planned to hit the same two or three key dates so that you can hold progress meetings for all concerned.

■ Publishing the plan

When you've finalised your plan, publish it . . . and wait for the squeals from suppliers. Tell them this is their last chance to complain. Once the schedule is agreed, excuses had better be good. Some companies include penalty clauses, but I feel this is usually counter-productive, as even a threat of enforcement leads to resentment.

■ Contacts

In addition, publish a complete list of contacts, containing everybody who has the slightest connection with the project. For each major activity, ensure that there are two names, and you have business, home and mobile telephone numbers. Email addresses and fax numbers are useful, but I have learnt not to rely on them, because you have no confirmation that the messages have been read and understood.

Then publish the schedule in chart form. Everyone involved should have access to a copy, and pin a big one up on your wall. Equally important, publish regular updates.

■ Monitoring Progress

The best plan in the world is useless if nobody takes any notice of it. Mark off each day on your wall chart.

It's a good idea to start an exhibition website. The chart can feature on it with a full specification of the stand. It can become an open forum for all involved in the production. But don't forget to protect the information against penetration by your competitors.

■ Acts of God and lesser deities

What happens if problems occur and deadlines are missed? However well you plan, you can't always allow for everything that might happen. Hopefully, your allowance for slippage will cope with minor acts of God.

Insist on being informed of any problems, however small, and, however difficult, be kind to the bearer of bad news. They are doing you a good turn. Try and anticipate difficulties and remember that they are usually cumulative. Where one thing goes wrong, it's almost certain something else will also go wrong there too. In the exhibition world, lightning strikes the same place not twice, but three or four times.

You can mark points of no return on your chart. The biggest will be on the stand build thread. What is the latest time that you can shift production to another builder if the one you've appointed proves incompetent? If things are looking a bit shaky as you near this date, lay it on the line with your builder. If there is any chance you are going to be let down, shift production to a reserve builder without hesitation. Don't submit to promises that you know in your heart will not be met. It will cost you dearly to shift, but not so dearly as missing the show or turning up with a shoddy, embarrassing stand.

■ Don't panic

Panic is your biggest enemy. So don't panic. Easily said, especially when the CEO is breathing down your neck and threatening you with your P45. Try not to lose control and blame everybody around you. Stop and think. If you don't come up with the solution within five minutes, bring in another person to help. It is very rare that a situation is entirely irretrievable, however bleak it appears at the time. There is usually somebody who knows somebody who can help.

Communications are the weak link when the worst happens. Sod's Law dictates that disasters strike on bank holidays or after six o'clock. So try to make sure there is a reserve for every key person and that their mobile numbers are always accessible.

Chapter 7

Outside the Frame

Not everybody exhibits at indoor exhibitions. There are lots of other opportunities to present your wares to the general public. In fact, anywhere that people gather and have time to wait, there you'll find a stand of some description. Anywhere customers can be persuaded to gather can be a productive venue for you.

■ Roadshows

Roadshows mean different things to different people, but generally speaking the principle is to take an exhibition round the country to the visitors' home towns rather than expect them to travel miles to an exhibition centre.

The theoretical advantages are obvious. Since they don't have to travel so far, people will be more disposed to attend. There will be fewer of them at each venue and they will have more time to spend with you. So runs the theory.

There are three major differences between travelling roadshows and static exhibitions.

- Because they are using smaller and use less well equipped venues, the number of exhibitors will be smaller and they tend to be the less prestigious suppliers. This makes them friendlier affairs.
- Since everything has to be moved every week or so, the stand and associated equipment has to be rugged and easily packed away.
- An exhibitor will probably have a permanent nomadic team assigned to the stand, although local reps might be called in to help.

Typical trade roadshows would promote graphics or catering equipment. The HR departments of large companies support careers roadshows. And there are roadshows promoting fitness equipment, holidays, DIY and golf supplies. The common factor is a clearly defined market segment within a reasonable hinterland. In the case of trade roadshows, one of an exhibitors' objectives would be to support local dealers.

■ Solus roadshows

Frequently a company will decide to go it alone. Motor manufacturers often do this to reach dealer staffs. They will stage a monumental new model launch in a fashionable and overpriced overseas resort for dealer principals, then travel a cut-down version round Britain to pass the message onto the dealers' rank and file.

Whatever type of roadshow you become involved in, the planning must be exemplary. While the contractor may still build the stand and take an interest in its maintenance, the question of logistics will probably pass to you. You will have to arrange transport, drivers, stand staff, accommodation and all the minutiae of looking after a travelling circus.

■ Production issues

Needless to say, anything that spends its life travelling round the country and being loaded and unloaded on a daily basis should be robust. It should also be light and manageable. The venues chosen may have poor access and getting parts in and out of lifts may be necessary. Also make sure that you have sack barrows and trolleys to help you carry components over long distances.

The search for perfect materials can lead to bizarre situations. Once on a roadshow, we had the bright idea of using honeycomb panels, just like those used for normal interior doors. The material was immensely strong, light and had a good surface. All went well, until we parked the truck containing the panels overnight next to the river at Lincoln ready to start building early next day. A mist arose from the water and by morning the panels were so warped that none of the bolt holes would line up. We just had to wait with the panels propped against radiators for them to return to normal.

■ The Dunkirk spirit

Be prepared for all eventualities. I have been snowed in for a week in Huddersfield . . . broken down miles from help high in the Pennines with a deadline looming . . . been waiting at Eastbourne ready to start only to learn that the contractors had hired a truck that was too small and nothing would arrive in time because it was too late to hire another one . . . built overnight for a major car manufacturer's dealer roadshow in a Glasgow hotel, only to be told in the morning that we had been allocated the wrong room and must move everything next door (the dealers were by this time drawing up in the car park). In every case, we got through it all, often not in the way planned, but certainly with satisfied clients.

What I have learnt over the years is that roadshows can be immense fun and great camaraderie builds up among crews and clients. In times of crisis all pull together and miracles are performed. If things don't always work out as planned in some far-flung place, nobody important from the company is usually there to notice. As long as the visitors are treated well and enjoy themselves and you meet the required levels of business, the roadshow will be a success.

■ Roadshow fleets

Exhibitors often either buy or lease a van and fit it out purely to transport the hardware and keep it safe. If the team is of any size, a battle bus might also be added, and the fleet painted in the company livery, the International Spigots' Demonstration Team. While a bus might at first glance seem hard to justify, it is infinitely preferable to taking individual cars.

■ Outdoor Shows

Often, when manning our stands in the stale, dull environment of exhibition halls in midsummer, we hanker for the outdoor life. We envy those companies at the county shows their sunshine and fresh air.

■ The downside

We conveniently forget the problems of pulling onto a grass field after a torrential downpour, when truck wheels find no grip and carve great gouges in the turf. We forget the gusts of winds that make pitching a marquee almost impossible and blow our brochures into the next parish. And we forget the inconvenience of either living in a caravan village or having to battle backwards and forwards with the show traffic along country roads to a hotel ten miles away. Outdoor shows are not a complete bed of roses.

■ The upside

They do have their compensations, of course. County shows are likely to be less intense. Visitors are not in so much of a rush and are there to enjoy themselves. However, don't fall into the trap that you too are there to relax and take it easy. If you have anything worthwhile to show visitors, you had better make it good as you are competing with a full programme of entertainment in the main ring. Off they dash to watch the excitement, then return, their enthusiasm refreshed, clamouring for stimulation.

■ Maintain standards

Neither, in the heady, friendly environment of fresh mown grass, trees in bloom and people in holiday clothes, should you let your standards slip. If you have an agricultural machinery stand, it should run as tightly as if you were at The Royal Smithfield Show. You are there to do business and make money.

■ Specialist outdoor shows

There are also strictly business outdoor shows for agricultural machinery, construction plant and commercial vehicles. The main purpose of these shows is to demonstrate machines in their working environment. In dry weather they are enveloped in clouds of dust and in wet they are knee deep in mud. In other words, enormous fun.

■ Hints about exhibiting outside

I have a few. Expect the worst possible weather. Then you won't be disappointed or embarrassed. Have your office under cover, and hire portable walkways and spare undercover storage facilities well picketed down against squalls.

If you are demonstrating machinery, carefully watch the Health and Safety Regulations, rope the area off and have alert stewards on hand. At county shows there are generally small children about who can't read warning signs and are attracted by things that are shiny and make a noise. Put guards over any holes that small children could crawl into.

Because everything is so accessible, the security problem is even more acute than normal. You don't have just normal thieves, if there are such things. You have souvenir hunters as well. They will take anything that's not bolted to something else or picketed down, just for the hell of it.

At night have somebody on watch. Vandalism is rife because it is almost impossible to maintain a secure perimeter.

■ Concourses and Malls

It's a logical concept. Instead of inviting people to come and see you, why not take yourself to where the people are? Great idea if you have something that will stop busy people in their tracks.

If you look for them, there are plenty of opportunities for truly solus exhibition sites. These are places where you have no competition for attention and literally thousands pass by. Sounds like an exhibitor's version of paradise? Maybe, but it's still hard work and there are downsides. Here are a few venues that you might approach:

- Shopping malls.
- Supermarket entrances.
- Railway, airport and bus station concourses.
- Foyers of entertainment and sports complexes.
- Town halls and public buildings.
- Pedestrian precincts.

In fact, any large public place where there is a constant flow or mass of people has potential. These sites tend to be most effective where the public have time on their hands, for example, while waiting for a train. Or better still, a plane. They are, however, suitable for products or services attractive to the public at large, the brasher the better. If you are offering something boring or with limited appeal, the sums will not add up.

■ Attracting people in a rush

Generally speaking, visitors don't stay long. They are on their way to somewhere else. If they pause, it is usually through curiosity or because you have tempting freebies to give out. The sales messages must be simple and direct. If you want to try and get their names and addresses, there has to be an incentive. If you don't have the resources to record their details on stand, hand out coupons that promise samples on redemption.

Since your relationship with visitors is fleeting and very basic, you will need quantity rather than quality of stand staff. Agency staff can learn all there is to know in ten minutes and will do a great job.

■ Trailers for Sale or Rent

The ultimate in self-containment is the purpose-built and equipped trailer. It requires a high investment and you have to be sure that you can get an adequate return from it, but often it's more than justified. It will give you great flexibility, being available for use at a moment's notice and able to go anywhere and set up quickly.

■ Conversions and custom builds

If you are thinking of converting one of your delivery 40-foot box trailers, it's doubtful whether it will be suitable. To start with, the floor probably won't be level and it will certainly be too high. A standard layout box body is too long and narrow to make a useful exhibition space, although it can be done. I have designed a mobile lecture theatre to seat 20 from one, with part of the space being taken up with a back projection booth.

Generally, planning and construction is a specialist job and the builders like to start from a low bed chassis. The structure is designed from the start to accommodate sliding extensions that can be moved out either manually or hydraulically. Often stairs are built in rather than relying on rickety steps that need a level base.

The design brief is a bit like turning the exhibition stand inside out. Outside, although it will be painted in the company livery, it will always be just a box on wheels. In most types, visitors enter and follow a predetermined path down the centre, with displays against the sides.

Another structure is rather like very posh burger bar, with visitors coming up long steps or ramp to a counter or a completely open side. This is more suited to a retail type of operation.

Chapter 8

Creature Comforts

Considering the average stand is on site for only three or four days, we expect a hell of a lot of it. We want it to be a workplace, a picture gallery, a communication centre, a hospitality unit and a demonstration area. We might also include within it a lecture theatre, a hands-on training area and a games room. It also has to survive a lot of rough treatment, especially if it is going to be used more than once. So it's not surprising that it can cost as much as a small house.

■ Colours and Finishes

Where do you start? I suggest by devising a colour scheme. This will usually be very much dictated by the company branding and corporate livery. However, it is often difficult to get a good match with normal decorating and furnishing materials. Corporate design manuals, the bibles in such matters, define colours in Pantone numbers, not the dove greys, Capri blues and sunrises of the paint charts in B&Q. However, times are changing and television DIY programmes have provided the stimulus for experimentation.

■ Neutrality

Unless you want to make a fashion statement, use neutral tones for walls, drapes and carpets. They won't offend and will allow your exhibits and displays to stand out. It is an oft-quoted mantra that you shouldn't have décor on your stand that you wouldn't have at home. You and your staff have to live there for several days.

The exception to this is if yours is one of those stands where you are selling over the counter. Here be as flamboyant as you like.

■ White

White looks fabulous on the first day, but soon shows the scuffs. If you must have white, avoid a matt finish that will not wipe clean. And if you simply have to have matt white, keep one of those little sample pots of emulsion in the cupboard for a touch up before you leave at night. Nevertheless, Apple for many years have used white to dazzling effect.

■ Metalwork

Structural metalwork is frequently used as a feature, being either left in its original anodised aluminium finish or painted in bright colours. Avoid neutral colours for such elements. They just look dusty and tired.

■ Woodwork

In my opinion, real, polished woodwork is the best way to impart an impression of quality. In contrast, imitation woodwork (e.g. laminates and paper foils) on a stand look cheap. You can also use different species of wood to give subtle tonal nuances. Sycamore and ash are light and ethereal, giving an impression of free thinking and lightness of touch. Beech is neutral. Oak and mahogany reek of establishment. They are solid and reliable. I would avoid pine as it looks too much like a 1970s kitchen . . . unless you want a 1970s kitchen look.

■ Finishes

There are many finishes for walls and flats, from flocked, like felt and suede, through textured, to plain paints.

Felts are very good if you are using light for effect. A neutral felt, while dull and lifeless on its own, comes to life with coloured gels and gobos projected onto it. Suede finishes look exceptionally good with chrome fittings.

■ Textures

Textures can be achieved in many ways. They can be applied directly to the surface, sprayed on or by using one of those spattering devices. Flecks can be incorporated in the process. Because texturing in this way is messy, it has to be done back at the contractor's works. So it's important to choose a texturing compound that is sufficiently flexible to survive the bending of panels when they are being loaded into the truck. However, contractors who use the technique regularly are aware of the best compounds and often have secret ingredients of their own.

Once the stand is up, they wear well, but can be difficult to repair. There are many textured surfaces available now that come on a roll or in sheet form. If you want to be adventurous, look at simulated corks, fabrics or scrims. In the right setting, plain hessian looks great and contrasts well with hi-tech elements.

■ Foils

Also available are metallic foils. These come in a wide range, from mirrors to brushed or stamped foils. Once again, to the imaginative mind they open up many possibilities. For example, a mirror finish can give depth to a pokey corner. On the other hand, remember that many visitors will find looking at themselves unsettling. A curved foil may also look uncannily like one of those distorting mirrors in fairgrounds with similarly distracting results. Use them sparingly for the best effect.

■ Paints

Paints are simple. Well, aren't they? For a very basic stand all you need is a can of paint, a roller and tray and dust sheets to prevent making a mess. Beyond that level, things mount up in complexity if we include all liquid finishes applied by brush or roller.

You don't have to stick with what's on the Dulux leaflet. Paints can now be matched exactly for tone, hue and shade. If your company uses Pantone colours in its corporate design handbook, these can be copied.

However, even though you know the colour to be accurate under white light, tungsten lighting on the stand and possibly reflected off other surfaces may make it look incorrect. Textures and grains can be incorporated into the paint finish. And with the popularity of television DIY programmes, manufacturers are pushing the technology to achieve ever more original effects.

■ Choose in the privacy of your own home

Designers vary in their attitude to finishes. Some have very strong views on what should be used in their creations, others will leave the final choice to you. You can have hours of fun looking through books of swatches. Many exhibitors do this with the designer or contractor present. Don't – their time is precious and you may be charged for it. Also a contractor will inevitably try to palm you off with overruns from a previous job or suggest a material they are trying to get a good bulk deal for that's being used on another stand on their books.

Cynical? Not me. If you can, take the swatch books away and do your dreaming back in the office with a colleague, or at home with your partner. Make a shortlist of what you like and then give your views to the designer and contractor. They will guide you by outlining any technical or aesthetic problems. There, some parts of exhibiting can be fun, can't they?

■ Furniture

One of the most infuriating aspects of the exhibition industry is the scarcity of good furniture that can be hired. I understand the reasons. Exhibition hire furniture has to be exceptionally rugged, it has to come in styles that suit all locations and it has to stack well in the warehouse and delivery truck. Those factors are all, however, for the hire company's convenience, not that of the exhibitor.

Upholstery comes in bright red, royal blue or grey scratchy fabric. The framework is tubular chrome. Great if you want to look like everybody else at the show. It is, of course, very practical and the catalogue gives you the exact dimensions. So it's easy to plan.

For those of you with friends in a furniture hire company, tell them not to panic. Although I complain constantly about the lack of choice, I shall be using their services for years to come. I, like most exhibitors, am too idle or too rushed to look for anything better.

■ Purchasing furniture

Some, however, make time and buy new for each show. You can argue that by going to a retailer like IKEA, it costs you very little more than hiring and you get a wider range to choose from. It probably won't be so rugged and be fit only for your daughter's bed-sit after the show. But think of the endless fun your staff will have opening the flat-packs and trying to work out the assembly instructions.

That is certainly one alternative. Yet another employed by a friend of mine is to watch for specialist auctions where they sell bankrupt stock. He buys cheap sofas and chairs that he can afford to have recovered in corporate coloured material. He is lucky in that he has storage space and warehouse staff to look after it.

■ Raised Floors and Ramps

Except for shell scheme stands, most reasonably sized stands are built on raised floors. This is because free-standing structures need anchor points and load-spreading feet, and to cover cable runs.

Show organisers and venues will usually insist that with a raised floor there has to be wheelchair ramp. This doesn't usually pose a problem, but it is something that must be allowed for in the stand layout. It's an expensive item to forget.

■ Using flooring creatively

For the adventurous, there are many creative possibilities with floors, and if you are thinking of laying one anyway you might consider something different. It would be difficult to justify for the normal trade fair, but for a fashion show, toy fair or a computer games exhibition, an illuminated disco type floor would generate buzz and excitement.

■ Split levels

Split levels are another device to create interest and form. Often this is necessary anyway in an auditorium situation, in order to raise presenters and rear rows of the audience to improve sight lines. If you are splitting levels, use curves if possible for aesthetic reasons. Also a curved edge to a raised area is less of a mental barrier. Once again, with split levels you may be required to provide ramps. If a level rises more than 10 cm, it's advisable to provide steps. With a platform over 15 cm, I would advise stanchions and handrails. Wherever there is a change in level, the edge must be made highly visible with a brightly painted strip or coloured tape.

■ Electricity, Telephone and Plumbing

Out of sight, out of mind. We all make the same mistake of taking services for granted. After you've been let down or had a major failure, you'll be a little more circumspect.

■ Eric's world

Everybody uses electricity. It comes to the stand in the form of an electrician invariably called Eric who is employed by the venue. He tells you that you have ten minutes maximum of his time and that according to his docket you want three power points, here, here and here.

So far so good, except that the requirements had to be submitted six weeks before show opening, and a good two weeks before you changed the plans. You now want four power points and you don't need one of the 'heres' any more. Don't worry. After a bit of job's-worthing and invoking excess charges, Eric compromises with four points, but not quite where you want them.

You think this is bad? You should have been around when the unions ruled with a rod of iron. Eric and his mates are to some extent justified, because every stand-builder in the hall, without exception, pleads the same sad story. Without exception, they are not only altering their electrical layout but are asking for more sockets. The electricians are magnanimous under this onslaught. They achieve miracles under extremely trying circumstances. At least that's what they would have you believe, but we in the business know that this always happens and they anticipated it all along.

◼ Spare a thought for the poor organiser

The organisers are no fools. They have to put in an estimate to the power company for their electricity requirements plus a big contingency. Experience tells them that if they can get you to commit early enough, they'll be able to charge you extra at an excess rate. One has to bear in mind that venues are often on a knife edge and have to watch the huge drain on the grid by large shows. Some shows are forced to shut down at half past five to avoid clashing with the domestic surge.

◼ Telephones

Telephone lines you may have to put up with, not for telephones but for Internet access. I prefer to rely on mobile phones for voice communications and if necessary have dedicated mobiles for the show. You can use them from the hotel after the show closes.

There have, however, been strange cases of happenings to mobiles at the NEC and other venues. The mobile poltergeist walks abroad. My mobile changed to Russian characters and others have had their memories wiped. It may be that there are intense bursts of microwaves in certain places at major exhibition centres. Honest, it's absolutely true.

With regard to the Internet, I suggest that if you want to demonstrate your website, use a simulation rather than a live connection. The web gremlins seem to love exhibitions.

◼ Plumbing

A quick word on plumbing. Don't! Not unless you really have to. Of course, if it's a catering or food show, there is no way out. Otherwise, use disposables.

Since I always call in an expert to do plumbing, I really know very little about plumbing at exhibitions, except that it makes a hell of a mess when it goes wrong. Then I walk out till it's fixed. So I don't know much about that either.

■ Carpeting

Do you really need a carpet? Strictly speaking, no. And I have heard it argued that stepping onto your carpet is a mental barrier to the casual visitor. Many stands work very well without, but I would suggest that you have one for the sake of your sales staff's feet, at least for that part where they stand. Aching feet are the biggest reason for them to sit down on the job.

■ Choice

There is usually more choice in carpet materials than in furnishing fabrics. You don't need anything of high quality for the short duration of the show. The contractor will show you swatches with literally hundreds of shades. I often wonder why exhibitors aren't sometimes a little more adventurous.

■ There's a lot you can do with carpets

A nice touch is to cut the company's logo into the carpet at the stand entrance. It's an unusual and effective way of branding that takes up no space at all.

Carpets can be laid under stand structures or around them. Obviously it is easier to lay a complete rectangle in one go. But be warned, you will make a mess if you go looking for plumbing leaks or cable runs after the structure is up.

Make certain that there is nothing to catch heels and trip visitors. If you are laying flat onto the hall floor, check that all the edges are taped down. Also make sure before leaving at night that none of the tape has risen.

■ Counters

Most stands need a counter. I would go as far as to say that the counter is where I often start when doing a design. That's because its primary function is to act as a focal point for enquiries and communications. It is the starting point for everything on the stand. A counter houses the telephone and is the place where sets of literature are given out. With a counter goes a receptionist. Normally it is manned either by a junior member of the exhibitor's staff or somebody hired in from an agency.

■ A workplace

Often forgotten is that a counter is a workplace. The receptionist, usually a normally proportioned person, may have to operate a laptop on the surface and will certainly have to write on it. So why make the counter so tall that the receptionist has to perch precariously on a high bar stool to reach anything? Also, allow enough space for the receptionist's legs. Many counters that I see are uncomfortable to operate for any length of time.

A counter can be prominent without having to dominate the space. Normally it doesn't have to be large. I have seen an original variation that worked well – a couple of cylindrical pods no more than half a metre in diameter at which two receptionists sat. We must remember that counters are administrative structures. Although it is a focal point, a counter should never distract from a demonstration or display.

■ Chat Areas

Some people like to stand to sell. Others feel more relaxed sitting. Most exhibition stands now seem to have a place, either in full view or in an enclosed area, where seated conversations can take place and serious enquiries are dealt with. There is always a psychological advantage in holding a business conversation with a seated customer. The very act of sitting seems to move the relationship on and taking somebody into an inner sanctum progresses it still further. There is a theory that a seated customer lowers his or her guard. Don't count on it.

■ Dog-legs

Chat areas seem now to have standardised into those dog-leg sofa layouts with coffee table in front. You know the type – just like most companies have in their reception areas. There really is nothing wrong with this arrangement, except that everybody does it and coffee tables are a bit of a menace on stands. They always seem to be in the way.

The disadvantage from a sales point of view is that it is difficult to face your customer. You sit on the skew. There is nothing to rest your clipboard on except your knee. Often dog-leg sofas can become real dogs.

■ Don't make it too comfy

Purists would ban such comfortable chat areas on the basis that, strictly speaking, there is no time on a properly organised stand for chatting. You are there to talk business and the very appearance of such a chat area sends the wrong message to visitors. In many ways I agree. I will explain later the principles of doing business on a stand. Without pre-empting this, I would explain that contact with business is based on the seven-minute standing pitch. Only when the visitor has passed this hurdle is he or she allowed to sit.

When you do invite your prospect to take a seat, what sort of seat should you offer? Let's look at what you do in your company when you have matters of serious business to discuss. Do you seriously seek out comfy chairs and plonk yourselves down in them? Of course not. You face your customer or colleague across a desk or sit at a conference table. The reason for this is that you need to be alert and be able to focus face to face. You also probably need to take notes. For these reasons, many exhibitors opt for small bistro type chairs and tables. They enable you to cross the 'sitting thresh-old' without falling into the trap of relaxing.

The other big problem with comfortable chat areas is that they encourage slackness in sales staff. Too often they will sit when they should be standing. Sometimes you feel that, after a hard night at the awards ceremony, they are about to nod off. On my stands, nobody, except the receptionist, sits unless they are with a customer and then only after they have passed the seven-minute pitch.

■ Enclosed Spaces

Here I'm talking about the chat area taken to the next stage. What I call the 'inner sanctum'. Given an adequate budget it is not enclosed on my stands, but on the first floor. The inner sanctum is where you share intimate secrets with special customers. They feel special because they have been invited inside and possibly wooed by coffee and snacks.

■ Treat your inner sanctum like an executive meeting room

Just as with chat areas, do not let either sales staff or customers relax too much in there. If you're not careful, they'll treat it as a welcome retreat from the hurly-burly of the show. The really professional way to use it is for salespeople to make appointments and book tables in advance. It can be done, and it gives a very good impression. And it is a very efficient way of moving half-intoxicated buyers out when their time is up. If a salesperson feels that the deal is too big to keep to the appointed time, it is worth taking to the bar or a private room.

You have already detected my aversion to sumptuous sofas and comfy chairs. In a enclosed area they waste even more space.

■ Cupboards

Of course you know what a cupboard is. A necessary place to put all the literature, samples, giveaways, coats, laptops, briefcases and general knick-knacks. You never have enough cupboards. Everyone will tell you that.

■ Halve your cupboard area

Stands have far too much cupboard area. It's dead space. If you can, reduce it by half. Find other places to keep all that stuff that doesn't need to be on your stand. Only have with you enough literature for the day in question. Keep the rest back in your hotel room. Salespeople who are there only for the day store everything in your cupboard rather than leaving valuable items in their cars in insecure car parks. It's understandable, but unacceptable. Five people's personal baggage takes up the space that would allow another visitor on the stand. Which is more important?

■ Security

It's always a problem with cupboards. Nothing on a stand is secure. Putting a padlock on a cupboard simply tells thieves that there is something valuable inside. And how often we see these only an arm's length from the aisle. It takes only a minute or so between security guard patrols at the dead of night to lever off a hasp. If you possibly can, take everything valuable away with you when the stand is unoccupied. At some venues, secure left-luggage cabinets can be hired by the hour or the day.

■ Literature Racks

How often do you see stands with stacks of literature left on counters, coffee tables and shelves? Valuable brochures and leaflets soon add to the general clutter and are easily knocked onto the floor. Rude visitors barge through waiting customers to grab brochures. What's more, leaflets all get muddled up together. What a shambles.

I guess that over half of stands make inadequate provision for displaying their literature. But why? When everything else is meticulously planned, how is it that so little thought is given to dispensing expensive print material?

The solution is obvious. Specially made racks and dispensers are not complicated to make nor are ready-made A4 plastic ones difficult to source from specialist suppliers. What they do, in addition to keeping the stand tidy, is make literature accessible and easily identifiable.

If you want to restrict the supply of literature only to visitors who ask for it, keep it behind the counter. There will be more about literature later on.

■ Flowers and Greenery

You either love flowers or can't see any point in them at all. There is certainly no point if they are not cared for. Very much the reverse. If you do have cut flowers, employ the florist to inspect, water and rearrange them every day. You are very unlikely to have anybody on the stand who has the expertise or the time to keep them looking fresh. Cut flowers should be placed where the comedians on your stand staff can't get at them, or you will arrive one day to find a bunch of stalks. Individual blooms will have been picked and presented to attractive visitors or put in their hair. (OK, I confess, I've done it too.)

I tend not to hire growing greenery unless there is a compelling reason to do so. The reason is simple. Potted plants are very attractive items and nobody notices when they disappear at the end of the show. If they all go at one time, your stand staff automatically assume the hirer has just collected them. Then a month later you receive a bill for £200 for plants not returned.

Chapter 9

Graphics

■ Principles of Graphics Communication

Every stand should tell a story. And it should attempt to do so in a logical sequence that can be understood by all. The telling of that story to exhibition visitors takes place in two ways, verbally and visually. We want it to be a story that to a varying extent will change their lives. When they come on your stand, you courteously greet them, converse with them, establish their needs and at least initiate the process of solving those needs – the normal oral sequence of selling. Most exhibitors get that right, more or less.

So why do so many companies lose the plot when it comes to visual communication? They don't seem to be able to put themselves into the shoes of passing show visitors. They find it difficult to imagine what a visitor's reactions might be.

■ Size isn't everything

Typically the first thing to greet you once you step aboard is a huge graphic panel with a headline like 'The Mark 22 Reciprocating Sprocket', followed by a photograph and technical specification. You look around and find that you are surrounded by other panels devoted to the Mark 18, Mark 36 and Mark 72, all variations of the same theme. There is no room for any other visual material on the stand.

The principle appears to be that if you have nothing much interesting to say, make what little you do say large. That will force people to read it. You wouldn't do that in a sales call, would you? What type of reaction would you expect if you burst into your customer's office, pulled out a big blow-up of your product and just shouted its dimensions and performance at him? If I were the customer, I know what I'd do.

Impact is, of course, important. Powerful, emotive graphics can arrest passers-by in their tracks. They can coerce them aboard through intrigue, passion and even sex. Just about every emotion has been appealed to within the bounds of decency and political correctness prevailing at the time.

As an exhibitor, once you have visitors on your home ground, you no longer need to shout at them. Try instead to use the same process as in verbal sales communication. In telling the story graphically, start by addressing the reader politely, then work your way methodically through the plot, ending by asking the reader to undertake an action.

Within reason, size is not the determining factor that makes people read or ignore a graphics panel. Provided visitors can see and read your graphics boards clearly and comfortably, interest is what encourages them to start reading. Brevity is what allows them to read to the end within their attention span. Simplicity is also vital. Not everybody at a trade show is an expert, least of all many in the decision-making chain who might stop by.

■ Positioning your graphics

Positioning is also important and to a large extent relies on common sense. Assume that your average visitor is 5 feet 8 inches (1.7 m) in height. The point of focus for a showcard or panel should be about one third of the way down from the top. The further an item is on your panel from this focal point, the less likely it is to be read and the less impact it will have. So don't leave your punchline to the end, which might be about navel height.

A comfortable reading distance is about half a metre. If you make your panel too big or outside the comfortable reading zone, the reader will move further back and take up more of your valuable stand space.

■ The communication sequence

I maintain that graphic panels on stands should follow the same communicating process as press advertising.

First, the 'lure'. Attract the readers' attention. It could be as simple as 'new', 'special offer' or 'free', long ago identified as the most powerful words in the copywriter's lexicon. Most trade exhibitors, I'm sure, would never stoop to such downmarket words, but you know what I mean. If you haven't any of those magic words at your disposal, and most of us haven't, examine your value proposition. Can it be put into a short, snappy phrase? Or possibly you could look to the unique selling proposition, the USP, of your brand or products. What is it that makes your offering uniquely attractive to your customers?

Once lured, intrigue, seduce them or empathise with them, so that they want to read on. Identify with their needs. Use the brand or product's USP, that single factor which makes it more desirable than its competitors in the eyes of your customers. Describe your product and the sales proposition.

End up by suggesting action. This is the visual equivalent of closing the sale, but it is unlikely that anybody will buy on the basis of visual evidence alone. So let's be realistic and suggest that they ask for a demonstration or book a factory visit.

Visitors feel more comfortable when everything is explained rationally, briefly and simply. They really do want to understand.

■ Branding

In all probability, you will have little control over how your stand will be branded. Everything will be laid out in the design manual. For visitors, used to seeing your ads in the trade press, passing your trucks on the motorway and buying your products off supermarket shelves, your stand must be instantly recognisable as representing your company. Its colours must be as close to the specified Pantone shades as possible, the logos must conform in shape and positioning, text in the approved fonts and even the staff should be dressed in clothes that identify them as belonging to your organisation.

I would submit it goes further. Everything about the stand must exude the essence of your brand. It should sweat the brand at every pore. If the graphic style is set out for you in the design manual, you must follow it, however tempting it might be to rebel.

In smaller companies there may be less rigid control, but the exhibition stand is not the place to express your independence. If you are unsure, get a good graphic designer with display experience to design your graphics and brief him or her to apply your brand standards to them.

■ What if you don't have a recognisable brand?

If yours is a company without a recognisable brand, have a ball. There is nothing like an exhibition stand for fixing a corporate identity in the minds of customers.

Where do you start? Nip round to that trendy design agency that's just set up in your town and arrange an appointment with the creative director. You will probably be quite shocked when you finally meet this exotic person to find that he or she has a shaven head and rings in just about every feature that protrudes from their face and body.

The brief you give the agency should be as full as you can make it. Procter and Gamble, in their guidelines on branding, talk about 'finding the consumer insight'. They seek to find what it is, beyond a product's performance, that will entice consumers to accept, like and buy it. In other words, what buttons in the consumer's perception do you need to press?

■ The creative explosion

Don't try to do the agency's job for them. The chances are that first time round they will totally ignore your brief and suggest for your conservative old engineering company something that would better suit a brand of jeans. Fear not. That is the way of creative people. They love to shock. Before stamping out in disgust, follow a well-tried process for such occasions. It's called 'examination by threes':

1 Question their reasoning and identify three key points.
2 Find the three things that you like most in their proposal.
3 Find the three things that most need to be addressed or improved in the proposals.
4 Ask for three very sketchy developments on what you've discussed.
5 Give them three days to come back with revisions.

This is being fair to them. The fault is probably yours in the first place for not briefing them properly or giving them the full facts. Put them under pressure and they'll respond. You'll be surprised when you see the next set of creative proposals. They'll probably be fairly near the mark.

■ Pictures

I don't know who first said it, but it's been round a long time: 'A picture is worth a thousand words.' It does, however, contain a deal of truth. The most powerful pictures express feelings that we could never put into words. Remember the Vietnamese girl, badly burnt by napalm, running from her village? Remember the looks of triumph on the faces of a winning team holding aloft the FA Cup? How can you put into words the tenderness portrayed in a mother's eyes as she feeds her baby?

■ Getting good pictures

Unfortunately in business we seldom have such striking and emotive images to show. It's difficult, I know, but there must be better pictures than most of those pasted on the walls of exhibition stands. The lack of imagination shown in choice of pictures is often unbelievable – aerial photos of the factory, office workers pointing at a computer screen, a photographic model pretending to be a rep on the phone, Olympic rowing eights, close-ups of hands shaking.

These pictures, straight from a stock photo library, aren't worth ten words, let alone a thousand. They are insincere and, even worse, plain boring. Before I am deluged by letters and emails from irate picture libraries, I would like to admit that I too use their pictures from time to time and that for certain topics, like faraway places, space and historic shots, they are indispensable.

There really is no excuse now for those boring pictures. Good professional photographers abound. Look at the space they take up in your local Yellow Pages. For pack and technical shots and portraiture you definitely need their expertise. But there is really no reason why you shouldn't have a go too. You might fail miserably, but on the other hand you might strike lucky.

■ Use your digital camera

Modern digital cameras offer high resolution, and with photo retouching software like Photoshop, an expert can make good many typical amateur faults. The great advantage is that you can take literally hundreds of photos to get just the three you want for the stand. I have heard that professional photographers, when called upon to illustrate an article in *National Geographic* magazine, will submit on average 700 photos for every set chosen for publication.

Why should your photos be better than those taken by professionals and supplied to the libraries? Simply because they capture reality. If you carry your camera with you all the time, you will be there when exciting things happen. You will be in the right place to grab the moment when the millionth armature comes off the line. You may be in the foundry just as a shaft of sunlight catches the sweat on the foundryman's brow.

I'm not advocating the kind of happy snaps that some of my clients frequently supply me to blow up for panels. You know the type – hot off the Boots production line with part of a thumb showing over the lens. I mean good semi-professional or club-standard photos that are within the capability of most of us after some expert tuition. Do an evening course or join a photographic society and learn your trade. Master the technicalities and find out what makes a great composition. The combination of expertise, imagination and opportunity should produce pictures that knock spots off those boring old library shots.

■ Corporate photo libraries

Of course, you could be in one of those unfortunate companies where you are given no choice. The pictures you must use are chosen for you by your design consultancy and listed in the design manual. This is the one occasion where I think branding can go too far. The images are supplied to you as files on a CD-ROM. The theory runs that, to stay 'on brand', all images must conform.

Unfortunately the design consultancy, in choosing these pictures, had in mind dreamy brochures and subtle advertisements. They confuse 'brand' with 'bland'. They never considered the use of such images on an exhibition stand, and, if they did, had little or no live experience of exhibiting. Many times I have been approached by a distraught client with a sheaf of wholly inappropriate pictures. 'Can you do anything with them?' they ask. The answer is no – well, not without causing excruciating pain to some poor graphic designer I have never met.

Exhibition stands are not really the place for meaningless giant blow-ups of commuter feet, atoms, close-ups of eyes, road junctions and power lines, unless you happen to be in the appropriate industries. There should be a government health warning – 'Say no to irrelevant mood shots!'

■ Logos

Logos equal branding. Correct? Not always. The concept that the more logos you can squeeze on a stand, the better it is branded is completely misguided.

Logos, where justified, should be powerful and dominating – for example on fascias – but used sparingly elsewhere. You really don't have to sign off every graphics panel with a company logo and strapline. If visitors don't know who you are by the time they start to read your panels, you've failed in branding the stand.

And if you can ditch the tiny 'TM's and 'registered trade marks' without the company 'brand police' noticing, do so. The Americans love them for some reason. Perhaps they never have to cut them out of polystyrene.

■ Copy and copywriting

Pictures may be more effective than words, but you still need words. There is still much that pictures cannot portray. A picture can convey an impression of speed, but it can't say how fast an object is moving. A close-up portrait of a model can show a flawless skin, but it can't explain the cosmetics and process needed to attain it.

Everybody admits that they use too many words. There is always so much to say and so little space to say it.

■ Key messages

Try once again to put yourself in a visitor's place. Imagine you are walking around a stand. I have talked about the way you, as that visitor, would be led through the story. But by the end of the visit, you want to take away a single message about the company and its products. You have 20 other stands that you must visit and countless others that might take your eye. Your brain has a limited capacity. You simply cannot retain all the 20 key messages.

On the other hand, that key message may not be the same for all visitors. A major customer might be interested in buying capital plant from you and they will be concerned about your standing in the industry and your resources. Another customer who is a local dealer may be more concerned with supplying spares and consumables. They will be more interested in your distribution. This means that if you are trying to communicate with these separate market segments, you should have separate graphics that they can go to and read. For each of these segments, however, there will be that single, memorable message.

■ Style

With regard to style, keep sentences and paragraphs short. Don't just replicate the copy from your ads slavishly. Reading a magazine is not the same as reading a showcard. An eight-word sentence and three-line paragraph are ideal. If bullet points help with lists, use them. Use a conversational style in writing. Visitors will find it friendlier and associate the copy more with talking to your stand staff.

■ Production

You could leave the production of your graphic panels completely to your stand builder, but I would advise against it for one very good reason. You need to exercise detailed quality control. Your stand builder is unlikely to notice if your logo is slightly off shade or pick up those infuriating spelling mistakes.

■ Allow plenty of time

Always allow much longer for production of graphics than you think necessary. The pitfalls are numerous. Be prepared for muddle and confusion, much of it caused by the very technology that was introduced to make life simpler.

■ The limitations of modern technology

Nowadays panels are composed complete on a computer using Quark Express or Illustrator. This is best left to an experienced designer. The problems arise when you want to approve proofs. Frequently you will receive files by email to approve. The wonders of modern technology make it all so convenient, don't they?

Well, no, they don't. You see, the file that will be sent you by email will probably be in PDF format. This can be sent in a variety of resolutions and normally is supplied with an RGB colour profile. This means that the colours used are red, green and blue, just like your television. The printer of the final graphic image may require CMYK, in which the four primary colours (cyan, magenta, yellow and black) of full colour print are used. The result is that the colours of the proof you receive will not match the final printer version.

The designer could send the image to you in an image format, like JPEG, but it will have to be compressed to get the file size down to manageable proportions for emailing. Quality is lost. Even if you have the same software that the designer uses so that you can view in exactly the same way that he or she does, it may only put in low resolution headers where the pictures are.

When approving graphic compositions like this, you have to take a view. If you don't want to pay for expensive colour correct proofs, and not many people do, you have to compromise. Perhaps get files run off in a couple of different formats, one for clarity and positioning, and one for colour.

■ Fonts

It doesn't end there. There is another problem that arises from time to time and has to be watched out for. It's known as 'fonts'. Surely Arial is Arial? Not necessarily. The Arial you use on your PC may not be exactly the same as that on the printer's Mac, and you only find out when, on your finished panel, you have several lines with one word in them. The printer's Arial is slightly wider than yours and forces a line turn.

Many companies have less common fonts specified by their design manuals. Your normal brochure printer will have disks full of every conceivable face, but the large-scale inkjet printer may not. Something similar will have to be substituted. If it's not close enough, you'll have to get on to your design agency to agree on a different one. You usually end up with Helvetica in one guise or another.

There is a simple solution. Take a trip down to the printer just before the panels are to be run off. View them on the monitor and check them thoroughly before the inkjet starts. It may be your last chance.

■ Copyright

It comes as a complete surprise to many exhibitors just how much of what they use on a stand is subject to the law of copyright. The law has changed fairly recently and you now have to wait until 70 years after the death of the artist or writer before his or her work enters the public domain.

It means that many things that we regard as old or traditional are actually still under copyright. If you want to use *Also sprach Zarathustra*, the famous track from the film *2001*, you might have the trustees of the estate of Richard Strauss after you. Although the music was composed in 1896, Strauss didn't die until 1949. I should, however, like to point out that I give full permission to quote from this work right now, provided you give me a credit.

Perhaps I'd better go through some of the items.

■ Pictures

To use any picture, drawing or photograph, you will have to pay the originator for its use. If you commissioned the work, you own it and normally have unrestricted rights of use. This may not always be so and there may be restrictions of use written into the originator's terms of business. Also the originator may want to retain the right to use the work as well, for instance in their own publicity.

If you use a picture from a library you buy from them a print or computer file for a set fee for the job you have in mind. You cannot then use it elsewhere. Alternatively, you can now buy whole libraries on disk with unrestricted usage. The disadvantage with the latter approach is that the good pictures get widely used, and you are quite likely to see the same picture on other stands at an exhibition. Of course, with pictures you take yourself, you are the copyright holder and you can do what you like with them.

■ Music

Most music on stands is used as incidental music on corporate videos. Check before using the video that exhibition use is covered for the parts of the world where you intend to exhibit. There is normally very little problem with trade fairs, but where visitors pay an entrance fee it will be regarded as use before a paying audience. Many stand-holders were caught at the Ideal Home Exhibition some years back.

■ Fonts and typefaces

Not a lot of people know this. The fonts you use on your computer are not there for you to use as you wish. The terms under which they are supplied specify for your own personal use. This does not cover print or broadcasting in any shape or form. You are expected to pay rights if you use them in the public domain. In a big company, the fonts specified in the design manual will almost certainly have been cleared by the originating foundry.

I doubt that, if you have transgressed, you will be arrested by the Font Constabulary. But cases have come to court, so it's worth bearing in mind.

■ Mounting

As you stand there watching your prints crawling off the inkjet, you will realise that a large print is a very unwieldy object. Unless you tell the printer otherwise, he'll probably just roll it up and pop it in a cardboard tube for you. Good for practising caber-tossing with. Very convenient for travelling on public transport, but not much use elsewhere.

Believe me, whatever the printer charges to mount it on a board, it will be worth it. There is simply nothing so frustrating as trying to paste down a print without wrinkles when you don't know how to do it. When you flatten one crease, another miraculously pops up somewhere else.

Unless you want to use the print many times, have it mounted on foamboard. This is a very stable mounting medium and very light, a boon if you ever have to carry ten panels from the car park and through three halls of the NEC to your stand. It is also worth getting the panels surfaced or laminated to protect them from marks.

If you want to reuse the panels, have boxes custom-made to fit them. You might even consider mounting on something a little tougher than foamboard. The main problems with some more substantial boards is that they are less stable and are apt to warp in storage or even overnight on the van.

Attaching panels to the stand is another source of frustration. If they are going to be used only once, no bother. But if you want to be able to remove them at the end of the show without damage, the best option is to use those tabs that work like Velcro. Blutack isn't really strong enough. In fact, with apologies to Blutack, I haven't found a use for it at exhibitions.

Chapter 10

Video and Interactive

There is nothing like a good video to stop the crowds – believe me. One that I produced for use at the Royal Smithfield Show some years ago was so successful that the organisers asked us to resite the screen as it was causing complete blockages in the aisle. Interactive workstations and touch screens don't have quite the same stopping power, but they can help greatly on an undermanned stand.

Please, try not to use your standard corporate video, tempting though it may be. The average length of corporate videos is far too great. Very few visitors can afford the time to watch eight or more minutes of generalities and puffery. It's well worth shooting something specially for the show, or at least editing down your existing material into something short and to the point.

■ Two types of video

There are two main types of exhibition video, one whose function is to grab people's attention and get them onto the stand, and the other to tell the story of a process, service or product application. Both should be succinct – the former probably no more than two or three minutes, snappy and to the point, and the latter up to a maximum of five minutes and more informative.

■ Loops

Where they run on a loop, there should be a clear break between performances, possibly of half a minute, to allow viewers to gather. Most will of course arrive half-way through and they should be encouraged to stay for a complete showing. This means that the average visitor wanting to watch a three-minute video right through will actually be on your stand for five or six minutes. One company I worked with slotted in one of its television commercials in the break.

Don't be lulled into the DVD trap. DVDs don't last for ever. In fact video libraries have found to their disgust that they don't last as long as old VHS videos: 12 to 15 plays, to be precise. So if you are taking the DVD route, get plenty of copies.

■ Auditoria

If you must have a longer, more leisurely paced video, possibly launching a new product line or covering a technical topic in some depth, build a small auditorium with seats or bum-bars. This will encourage visitors to relax and concentrate on what you have to say. In such circumstances, it's worth having a steward to inform passers-by that a performance is about to start, to usher them into the auditorium and to direct any viewers who look interested towards a rep.

■ Video standards

I'm often asked what video format 'can I get away with?' My reply is that on an exhibition stand you can't get away with anything. The difference between a showing on your stand and in your board-room is that in the boardroom the viewer sees the video just once. On a stand it will be watched many times and any imperfections that slip by on the first viewing are noticed on subsequent viewings. Almost always it is your competitors who notice faults first and will stand embarrassingly in the aisle discussing them in audible tones. Poor-quality copies become particularly irritating.

The situation is becoming even more confused by differences of opinion over what constitutes broadcast quality. For a long time, Beta SP was an acceptable standard throughout the industry, which was great. But it is becoming increasingly difficult to find the relevant Beta facilities, especially in certain countries abroad. DV, and equivalent digital formats, are taking over and have the big advantage that there is no loss of quality with the generations. DV and MiniDV tapes are now generally accepted in both PAL and SECAM as being broadcast quality, but unfortunately the NTSC version is not. There is no difference in visual quality between DV and MiniDV, and the difference in sound quality is unlikely to be detected in an exhibition environment. It's high time we dropped VHS as a medium for anything except editing and home use. It really isn't good enough today.

The digital video revolution has, of course, opened up vast areas of possibility for exhibitors. In theory, almost anybody can buy a small DV camera very reasonably and edit on a laptop. But a word of caution. Video production, though fun and creatively stimulating, does require considerable expertise in camerawork and editing. To start with, although the DV format is certainly up to the job, the lenses on home video cameras generally aren't. However, semi-professional models aren't expensive to hire, nor are they difficult to use. Any normal eight-year-old should master the technology in about half an hour. Anybody over 30 might take a bit longer. Gifted amateurs can produce gems, but the standard of most home-produced videos on stands is abysmal. If you want to do it, go on a course or bring an expert in to help.

■ Sound advice

Voiceovers and music on looped videos can – no, almost certainly will – become a major source of irritation after the fiftieth time of listening. I have often arrived at a client's stand on the second day to find that their expensively produced video is showing with the sound turned off. Sometimes neighbours have complained or the track has taken the guise of a new form of Chinese water torture for the stand staff.

If you feel a voiceover is absolutely necessary, have the artiste deliver the words slowly and clearly, so that they can be heard without the volume having to be too high. Foreign visitors for whom English is a second language will really appreciate simple, concise wording. With music, stick to middle-of-the-road tracks that don't interfere with or annoy anybody else. Your staff will find that with a bland track the ear is able to filter out the music after a couple of hours and hardly notice it.

■ Monitors and Plasmas

Plasma and flat screens have all but taken over from the old CRT versions. After all, who would choose something like the old telly that you used to watch *EastEnders* on in preference to a sexy thing that looks like a shiny black paving slab? Strangely the diverse flat screen technologies have not progressed as fast as we were led to believe they would. Some years ago, we were told that screens as thin as paper that could be unrolled from a tube, pinned on a wall and plugged in were just around the corner. There have been other corners and the concept seems no closer to production.

One problem we have at the moment is that although screens are becoming larger, the resolution of video has not improved, unless you spend a small (or large) fortune on high definition TV. There is still a hefty premium for HDTV, but the cost is dropping fast. This means, for the moment anyway, that if you have a larger screen you must allow viewers to move further away. On the other hand, plasmas and LCDs can be viewed over a greater arc.

If you want screens to be seen from the aisle, they really need to be high and visible through a wide arc. This frequently poses problems, since they are heavy and need a substantial structure to support them. In such situations, the most practical solution is to suspend them from a robust truss system like Trilite.

■ Rear Projection

An alternative is a rear projection booth. Most companies now have small data projectors and they are ideal for this purpose, provided the lumens level is high enough for the location of your booth. Booths can be specially built or hired. I prefer the latter, because you know that they have been made for the job and the optics will be right. Mind you, I have shown films on stands using simple mirror tiles, which proves that the quality of the mirror isn't critical.

If you really want to go to town, there are pro-cubes and video walls to tempt you. Here you certainly have to watch the quality of the master. You can use the bank of screens to show a conventional video, or alternatively you can use them creatively. Programme individual screens separately so that several programmes are run simultaneously. If you can justify the cost to do this, call in an expert.

■ Workstations

What a great idea, they say. Let's put our website on the stand. All we need is a PC, monitor and landline. They're right, it really is a great idea and there are many other uses for a PC on site, both for marketing during open hours and for administration after the doors have shut. But it takes a little organisation and forethought.

■ Security

The greatest problem is security. Not just from having the stuff nicked, which happens often enough, but letting unsupervised foreign fingers loose on your mouse and keyboard can result in competitor sabotage and other nasty practices.

The moral? Keep all computers carefully supervised and build firewalls like you are playing Mah-Jong. If you are at all worried, develop a touch screen version of your presentation.

And talking of things getting stolen, try to dissuade stand staff from bringing their laptops. Public exhibitions especially are full of people for whom the temptation of a laptop left propped up against an exhibit is just too much to resist. There really isn't any use for a loose laptop on a stand.

■ Types of workstation

Workstations seem to have evolved into two types of installation. The first is the flat counter, with several machines spread along it. It's easy to make and the cable runs can be hidden. The second is the stand-alone unit. You can make it yourself, but there are many very attractive ready-made units that can be hired. Unless you have very strong views on the matter, my advice is to hire one or more of these. They are hardwired with all the things you need.

When you hire PCs, as many exhibitors do, bear in mind that they come normally with just the operating system loaded. You might, if you are lucky get Microsoft Office thrown in, but the rest you'll have to install yourself and remove afterwards. A word of warning here: check that your software licence covers the requisite number of computers used on site. Remember, you are on view to the world at large, and who knows, the licence police might be on the prowl. I haven't heard of anybody being caught, but don't say you weren't warned.

■ Websites on stands

Nowadays everybody wants to show off their websites at exhibitions. Heaven knows why. If you have to show your website, don't do it on-line. Produce a simulation. I would not have any link from a stand to my company network, however well it is supervised. The risks are just too great.

Not so long ago, Apple themselves caught a virus on the stand network, amazingly enough through a CD produced as a show guide. Apple had removed all their security software to make their machines run faster. I don't know if they were linked back to base, but if so it could have proved catastrophic.

Chapter 11

'Let Me Enterain You' – Presentations, Demos and Live Elements

'Roll up, roll, up! Come and see the amazing MX300! See it put through its paces! Feel the vibrating metal and handle the superb products!'

The barkers of Victorian times knew how to drum up an audience. Maybe we are too sophisticated to respond to such techniques today. Maybe not.

There is nothing quite like a live performance for attracting interest, and to have things that work on a stand and people to present them indicates commitment and self-confidence. A well-devised presentation or demonstration also takes pressure off the sales staff, since they don't have to spend time describing products and how they work. They can then concentrate on the primary task of building customer relationships.

■ Objectives

As with every aspect of exhibiting, consider the objectives first, and certainly before hiring loads of expensive gear. These are questions you should be asking: What is the single most important message that your presentation or demonstration needs to get across? Is it speeding up a process, increasing quality, or reducing costs? Whatever it is, focus on it.

'Good news, I could let you have one of the new MX300s for your stand at Componex,' says Keith Thompson, the works manager, as he bumps into you in the corridor one day. 'That would be one in the eye for Allied Grubscrews and the Argonaut has given his blessing.'

You bet he has. The Argonaut doesn't have to make it work. Anything to get up the nostrils of Allied Grubscrews has his support. Any chance to score points over the toffee-nosed old Harrovian MD of his arch competitor. And you detect that maybe Keith is looking for a chance to spend a week at Componex and get his podgy snout into the trough of corporate hospitality.

■ Consider at length

Wisely, you put off any snap decision. Good. Think long and hard before embarking on a live demonstration with machinery, catering equipment or hand tools. They are only one level below animals and small children as recipes for potential disaster. At their best, demos are wonderful to behold. They attract large crowds, retain the audience's attention and present the company's case professionally and memorably. At their worst, they are abysmal. Unfortunately the bad outnumber the good.

The starting point must be to return to that single most important message. Then work out how the story you have to tell can be made into an enthralling presentation that will justify visitors stopping and giving you their attention for ten minutes. If it isn't immediately clear, skip this section.

If you think your story is a worth telling or are determined to do it anyway, the following tips might prove useful.

The first principle of presentations and demos is that there are no substitutes for planning, site visits and off-site rehearsals. Leaving any single factor until you arrive at the finished stand is too late. Believe me, demo machines are prima donnas. They are glamorous, temperamental and expect respect. However, with the right preparation, they can be glorious.

■ Planning the Show

The biggest mistake most exhibitors make is that their presentation or demonstration is too long. There are two types you could try.

■ The short approach

The first is a short, punchy affair designed to stop passing traffic and hold its attention. There should be sufficient space on the stand to sit or lean while watching. If there isn't, you risk complaints of impeding the traffic flow.

Five to eight minutes is the most that will hold the attention of casual visitors. Any longer, and they will start to either drift away or lose interest. A benefit of these short presentations is that they can be re-run throughout the day with just a few minutes needed to reset the equipment and allow the presenter a cup of coffee.

■ The prestige approach

If you want something grander, a prestigious affair that lasts longer, I would suggest a more formal, self-contained auditorium. Better still, hire one of the many suites attached to the hall. Because you are asking visitors for a greater commitment, run an advance booking system and tell them what the presentation will be about and how long it will take. The self-contained auditorium on the stand is only practical if you have masses of space. You need to reconcile yourself to the fact that it will probably be used for only a couple of hours a day. The rest of the time it is dead space.

■ Machine cycles

I acknowledge that as stand manager, you have little control over how long a machine takes to perform one production cycle. It's not the fault of the machine or the engineers. Performing at exhibitions isn't its prime function. So do a dummy run off site to check the timings. If it takes too long, you'll have to find ways round this. Unless the time taken to complete a cycle is a major selling feature, cheat. Nobody minds if you get the message over and don't pretend it's for real.

■ Consumables

Ensure regular deliveries or adequate storage of raw material so that the machines don't run out. Equally, make sure you can dispose of finished products. Maybe these can be distributed as samples. If not, bulk disposal may become difficult as the organisers will not want fork-lifts moving about during the show. In all probability, it will mean storage on the stand for raw materials, finished product and waste sufficient to last from opening in the morning until after closure in the evening. With several machines on your stand, you may have severe problems.

■ Technical support

Make sure that you get full technical back-up. Your company's machines were never designed to be run under exhibition conditions. They normally have permanent solid beds, clean power and long operating cycles. At the show, they will probably be mounted on temporary bearers, be subject to surges as other machines are switched on and off, and will be run up for short demos then run down.

There may not be sufficient space for adequate cooling and the need to keep them looking clean may result in running them at low lubricant levels. The only way to keep up a busy schedule of demos is to have maintenance engineers in attendance all the time.

■ Health and safety

Health and safety are important with demonstrations. Not only are you exposed to inspection all the time, but you are surrounded by visitors, many with little sense of self-preservation. You wouldn't believe what the general public are capable of. If children are admitted, as at agricultural shows, you have my sincere sympathies. I shall tackle these issues later.

■ Scripts

Scripting a demonstration is difficult, partly because the audience is diverse. Some visitors will be experts, but the majority won't. Always err on the side of simplicity, even if your target audience are professional buyers. Demos look pathetic when there are just two or three spectators.

When writing the script, try to keep the tone conversational. Too often I have had to rewrite a client's scripts that were just expanded versions of the copy from the brochure, dry as tinder and full of jargon.

■ Describe what the machine is doing

The presenter should describe what is happening out of sight, not stating the obvious. There is no need to say, for instance, 'Now I press the switch.' If you want to draw attention to the switch, mention its benefits: 'The switch is conveniently placed at the top of the console,' or 'The loading tray is adjustable, so you can load in bulk from a palette or by hand for small runs.'

■ The 'U' factor

Use the word 'you' as much as possible to encourage the audience to 'own' the machine. Draw them into the demo as much as possible. Get them to compare with what they are having to suffer back at the plant. Ask questions, like 'What would you do with your existing machine at this point?' or 'How long would this normally take you?' It lets them highlight their dissatisfaction with what they have now and identify with the benefits of the MX300.

■ Verbal branding

Branding is just as important in speech as it is visually. When talking about the machine, use its name. Rather than 'This machine is 20 per cent faster than its nearest competitor,' say, 'The MX300 is 20 per cent faster than its nearest competitor.' Don't be coy about your new machine. Keep referring to it by name long after it sounds over-repetitious to you. Many of your visitors will never have heard of the MX300.

Make sure the MX300 has an identity that will be remembered. Unfortunately, technical products tend to have numbers rather than names. Years ago the MX300 would have been called the 'Gearmaster', or if the marketing manager was an eloquent type, the 'Phoenix' or 'Panther'. Now it's much more difficult, with titles that remind you of algebra lessons at school.

In the script, draw verbal pictures. Give your product personality, and encourage people to visualise it in their premises. 'Just imagine, sir, what the saving of half a metre in length will mean in your factory. Possibly you can fit in a conveyer head where there wasn't room before.'

■ Price?

Do you mention price in presentations and demos? In principle, no. That is the domain of salespeople rather than presenters. In practice, price is often a key part of the package. But keep it to last. If you make a good case for quality and performance, a high price will be justified. Conversely, a low price becomes 'exceptional value' rather than just 'cheap'.

■ Maintain momentum

Machines never run conveniently for commentaries. There will always be long periods when nothing seems to be happening. You mustn't lose momentum. The skilled scriptwriter uses these periods to recap on what has just happened or to describe what is going on out of sight in the heart of the machine.

■ Visual support

If you have a live, fire-breathing machine gobbling through mountains of steel blanks at one end and spewing out sprockets by the thousand at the other, do you need visual support? Sometimes it is sufficient to say what you see is what you get. Normally, however, you need to spell out the performance in a form that will be memorable. And this means some form of screen or screens with graphics.

■ PowerPoint

Simple PowerPoint presentations are adequate in most situations and are very cost-effective. If you don't feel sufficiently competent to do something professional, call in a specialist designer. Even if your conference production company or PR agency want to promote their own highly sophisticated presentation software, I would ask them to use PowerPoint, since it is used everywhere and you can always find somebody local to operate it or make changes in a crisis (this is probably the very reason why conference producers don't want you to use it).

■ Celebs, Major and Minor

So much for demonstrations. What about other live elements? Celebs, maybe. A big name from television or films will really put the company on the map, won't it?

■ A cautionary tale

Perhaps. Here's a nightmare scenario that actually happened. Only the names have been changed, to avoid myself and the publishers being sued.

You discover a month or so before the show that the Argonaut's cousin is a sister of Geri Halliwell's best friend. Wouldn't it be great if he could arrange to have a real celeb like her to visit the stand? Naturally you agree. Who wouldn't?

But is it such a good idea? And how do you make the most of the opportunity if it comes off?

The MX300 has very little in common with Geri. There is no association between them, so it would be hard to justify her presence on purely business grounds. Her presence on your stand will only attract a host of the feeble-minded with little serious business at the exhibition. But naturally Jason the Argonaut doesn't see it that way. It would mean another photo to stick up on his office wall beside the one of him shaking hands with Denise Van Outen at a charity function.

Of course, the inevitable happens. Geri is already booked, but her best friend suggests an alternative who has appeared briefly on *Big Brother*. Jason has never heard of the girl but is taken in by a persuasive press release from Max Clifford's office. The C-list personality is booked. Then a news story is broken about her sordid affair with a randy politician. All the intimate details appear in the *Sun*. She will not cancel the contract and is determined to appear, convinced that it will provide a photo opportunity. It possibly doesn't occur to her that a photo op in the engineering press will do little for her career, nor that the paparazzi from *Hello!* might be giving Componex a miss this year.

■ Celebs out of control

Cases of celebs biting the hand that feeds them are too long to list. Just consider the famous footballer hired by a razor company who decided one day to grow designer stubble, or the Blue Peter presenters caught taking drugs at parties. Get a good solicitor to draft the agreement before parting with your cash.

Here's another one that happened to me. We hired a well-known television presenter because his catchphrase fitted our products. What we overlooked was that one of our major trade customers was owned by Plymouth Brethren, who never watch television. The promotion meant absolutely nothing to them and they weren't keen to take the associated in-store merchandising.

Then there was the famous radio announcer who arrived almost paralytic . . .

Enough said on this subject, I think.

■ Entertainers

Exhibitors come up with all sorts of entertainment on their stands to attract attention, from pole-dancing to body-painting. Some are staged set-piece events, say once an hour for ten minutes. Others run continuously through the day. Yet others are there to support a one-off celebration. Anything is fair game in the search for originality.

But they have to be of a high standard. Don't employ the financial director's nephew as a ventriloquist to return a favour. Go to a top agent to get the best and be prepared to pay for it.

Attractions can be crowd-pullers. One company regularly includes a simulator ride.

This is very different from the use of celebs, whose sole function is to gather crowds. Entertainers can do that, plus help to tell your product story or enhance the branding. What's more, if you are clever, you can get them to spread your messages far from your stand by wandering around the show.

A superb example of the effective use of entertainment was when I was asked to write a script for an escapologist hired by an electronic device manufacturer at the Mac Users' Show. The concept was of a race between the dangling escapologist escaping from straitjacket, various chains and handcuffs, and the company's device at performing its task. Not only was it a real crowd-stopper, but it carried a very powerful message – the device beat whatever competition it met by doing the task in under four and a half minutes.

Examples of the creative use of entertainment are:

■ Jugglers.
Jugglers are great because most people at some stage have had a go at it. So the public can empathise with a good juggler. Also jugglers are easy to brand. Not only can they wear something

corporate, but if your product is suitable, like bottles of fruit juice, they can juggle with them as well. Even juggling balls can have logos applied to them, although in my experience they soon wear off.

- **Mime artists and human statues.**
  There is very little in the field of human endeavour that mime artists will not try and mimic. If you are marketing food processors, what more entertaining introduction can you have than two chefs miming how it used to be. They will involve bemused passers-by by asking them to hold imaginary utensils and look at make-believe scales to ensure that the quantities are right. Human statues have a similar effect and are great crowd stoppers when they wake up.

- **Magicians.**
  Close up magicians can be very successful at engaging small groups of passers-by. As with jugglers, their props can be customised and with some ingenuity simple brand messages can be conveyed.

- **Walkabout costume characters and stilt-walkers.**
  Tremendous value, especially if the organisers have no objection to them wandering freely. They can distribute samples, invitations or competition entries throughout the hall and take your branding with them. If you want to take the concept still further, engage one of the hilarious comedy teams like Mischief La Bas, the Natural Theatre Company or Dot Comedy. They can get your messages over in far-flung corners of the hall you would never otherwise reach as well as bring welcome humour to a dour event.

- **Musicians.**
  If you have an auditorium, why not use it when no formal presentations are taking place? A string quartet or harpist are ideal. They won't offend the neighbours, nor will they distract from the serious business you are trying to conduct. While I have never tried this soothing approach, I am assured that visitors often remark favourably about it.

- **Cartoonists.**
  Cartoonists are great because they are able to offer something that visitors will not only take away but probably hang on their office walls. The secret here is to make sure that there is a discreet logo on the corner of every sheet of sketching paper.

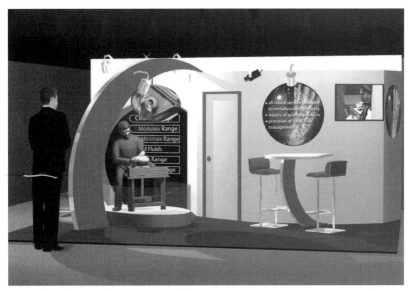

When there was no product to demonstrate, a potter provided a focus point

- Balloon modellers.
  Definitely not suitable for most shows. Who wants to cart around an unwieldy and embarrassing rubber Bugs Bunny all day? If there are children present, however, balloon modellers will have visitors beating a path to your door.

Presenters

Presenters come in all shapes and sizes. You can hire somebody who is good with words, possibly an actor from the local rep or a minor anchor person from a television station. They are ideal for non-technical subjects or for interviewing in a two-handed session with your technical director.

A word of warning. Never try to imply that an actor is one of your technicians. If the story is a technical one, it is easy to detect when an actor is just mouthing something totally incomprehensible to them. In this case, you could employ a technical presenter, possibly a university lecturer.

Why not use one of your own staff, as long as you don't expect the equivalent of a Royal Shakespeare Company actor? You might be lucky and find that you have a very accomplished speaker among your colleagues. Even if not, nobody will mind too much, as long as they are reasonably confident. If everything is done honestly and with integrity, it should be fine. Content is more important than style.

Professional presenters should work without a script, but members of your own staff may not be so confident. It may be advisable to have a lectern for them to rest their notes on, but don't allow them to read off a script. They need eye contact with the audience.

If your presenter is also expected to operate a PowerPoint presentation, a remote keypad will be necessary. Always have a technical rehearsal, with a full run-through of the slides, and make sure the presenter is completely comfortable with the cue points. Impress on them that if anything goes wrong, they should stop and wait for help rather than try to muddle through.

Very few presenters, professional or amateur, are able to demonstrate machinery and maintain a commentary at the same time, so it is usually better to split the task.

■ Hands On

A frequent question I am asked is how to get audience participation at presentations. It is indeed difficult, mainly because presentations need to be tight and controllable. Audiences, with the best of intentions (and occasionally with less well-intentioned motives), are uncontrollable. Here are some ideas you might try.

■ Keypads

These are the same as used at conferences. Linked electronically to a computer, they give the audience a chance to vote. The computer immediately transmits the results of the poll to a large screen. The keypad system can have great impact, and the data collected over the duration of the show might be very valuable. A security caution – keep an eye on the audience. For some reason keypads, even when attached to cables, seem to be attractive to certain individuals.

■ Simulations

Some industries lend themselves to computer simulations, and even ones that don't can often devise simple games that can be used to demonstrate a sales point.

■ Beam Me Up, Scotty

Satellite and other links are a great idea for involving people from around the world. I have seen them used to bring a keynote speech from a CEO in the States down to a stand in Birmingham, to co-ordinate product launches at stands around the world and even to beam in from Tokyo an important sporting event sponsored by a Japanese company to satisfy its senior executives who were at an exhibition. What we Europeans thought of this did not worry them in the slightest. They cheered just as if they had been at home.

It occurred to me that with a little foresight these live satellite links were unnecessary. There was really no need for the American CEO to go out live. His address could have been pre-recorded and distributed at far less cost by other means.

Now things are evolving quickly, with broadband connections and other advances in communications. If we can't quite get the quality we need through a live Internet connection yet, it is only a short step away. Even though we can't quite manage to transmit high-quality images live, it is commonplace to send files over the Internet in AVI, Quicktime or MPEG formats to be played out immediately downloading is complete.

We are so used to transmitting live images via mobile phones and home PCs that the concept has become mundane. It has lost its magic, even though we watch low-resolution images, with dropped frames and a delay.

If you want to go down this road, contact a specialist company. They will advise on the latest technology and guide you through the process relatively painlessly.

■ Rehearsals

Time spent in rehearsals is seldom wasted, and there is nobody so expert or knowledgeable that they don't need criticism. Rehearsals are the key to first-class presentations.

Don't wait until you are on site. Write your script in good time and get your presentation staff and demonstrators together back at base. It is best to agree the words before the pressure is on.

■ Auditoria

Auditoria. Places to go to listen to things. And, although technically outside the strict definition, watch things taking place. Auditoria are the tables at which we feast our senses of sight and hearing.

They are high investment features. They occupy a lot of space and are only functional for a small proportion of the time. So they just *have* to work.

We as audiences will concentrate on what is being said and shown us only if we have no distractions or obstructions. That is sometimes difficult on a stand surrounded by noisy neighbours. Although the presentation may last only ten minutes, our minds will still wander if we suffer pains in our behinds, are unable to see properly or have to strain our ears to hear.

■ Podia

A presenter has to be seen. If you think there will be any difficulty, build a raised stage or podium. It is relatively easy to work out the sight lines beforehand with a pencil and ruler on a sheet of paper. Allow for people of below average height.

■ Seating

The main object of seating in an exhibition auditorium is to position the audience in the best place to view a presentation. There is little need to make them too comfortable as they won't be there for long. If you want to seat more than six to eight, the seating should be fixed. If you want to save space, use a bum-bar.

Chapter 12

Marketing Your Stand

■ Invitations and Incentives

Once you've gone through all the pain of getting your stand built and installed, you want the world to know about it. Well, at the very least you want your customers to know about it. You can't leave to chance their finding you or they may miss you completely at a big exhibition. They might even arrive at your place when they have no time left to talk. The answer is to invite them in good time, telling them about what awaits them when they visit your stand – seeing that new range of rocker valves you are so proud of, or meeting the new sales manager who has taken over the territory.

■ 'Must have' invitations

I get loads of invitations to stands. Most get tucked away in a file somewhere. There is in the main nothing much wrong with them. It's just that they don't inspire me. I don't throw the invitations away because I realise just how much sweat and toil has gone into the stand's production. I merely file them, just in case I have an odd half-hour at the show with nothing to do. Of course, that never happens.

A very few invitations are special, however. They qualify for the 'must visit' category. Looking back at past performance, the reasons why these are successful are:

- They are personal, from friends or people I know and respect.
- The exhibitor has something of value to tell me and informs me of the benefits.
- The invitation is so original that it intrigues or makes me chuckle.

The first reason is the most compelling. I feel flattered and honoured to be remembered. Frequently there are personal invitations from senior company directors I have never met (and probably never likely to meet). I have no problem with this, but I really appreciate it when the salesperson who is my contact with the company attaches a brief personal note or rings to check that I will be coming.

A good tip is to make the invitation easy to carry. I find that when I'm at a show I have bags of brochures, so invitations that fit the pocket are easy to find.

■ Complimentary tickets

Some exhibition organisers give exhibitors a number of complimentary tickets, or allow them to buy tickets at an attractive discount. These are great to include in a mail shot or supply to the sales force to distribute.

■ Incentives to visit

At the exhibition itself, why not offer visitors a real incentive to visit? A chance to win a substantial prize, a free gift or an invitation to lunch. Incentives are generally very effective ways of attracting people to your stand. Abbey National Properties, whose logo used to feature a multicoloured umbrella, used a very effective device to attract visitors. At the entrance all visitors were handed a card bearing just the outline of the umbrella and simple instructions. Four girls toured the exhibition floor, each with sticky paper colour segments to be stuck into a space on the outline on the card. A visitor had to find all four girls to complete the umbrella. A completed card, plus of course the visitor's business card, could be exchanged at the stand for a real Abbey National umbrella. The scheme proved so successful that the supplies of umbrellas ran out before the end of the first day and the company had to be scoured for additional umbrellas. The bounty of contacts and leads was valuable and kept the marketing department busy for some time.

■ Advertising and Public Relations

If you book space at a major exhibition, one of the first things you will notice is the sudden interest in your welfare from salespeople selling space in the trade press.

'How are you, then? Haven't spoken to you for some time. Lucky I've caught you. Have I got an offer for you!'

Before you have a chance to imagine the extent of this good luck, you are told that *Sprocket News* is publishing a special, bumper show edition. It will become a major reference for the whole industry and will be kept on buyers' desks for the whole of the coming year. You are being offered a quarter of a page of editorial and the facing page is reserved for your advertisement.

'It's a wonderful opportunity, and I've got two other companies practically snapping my hand off to get that space. I'm afraid you'll need to reserve it now to be sure. And here's the best part. Since you've taken 12 insertions over the year, I'll knock 15 per cent off the standard rate and waive the special edition and facing matter premiums.'

How nice of them to think of you thus, and with such a generous offer. But hold on a moment. You are entitled to the 15 per cent as series rate anyway. And the editorial will be little more than a paragraph in what is effectively a pretty boring catalogue. Is it such a great deal? It depends on the show, the publication and if you have something special to tell show visitors.

■ The 'special' show edition

It's a peculiar quirk of human nature that whenever someone undertakes a major enterprise, there will be host of business people ready to take advantage of it in their own way. At every trade fair there will be trade journals trying to cash in by publishing features and supplements. These vary greatly in quality and interest. Some provide little more than a map and list of exhibitors. Others really push the boat out and do industry reviews with informed comment and sheaves of useful statistics. Some of the latter type of publication available on bookstalls produce volumes so full of interesting editorial matter that their circulations increase considerably at show time. The fat Farnborough Airshow editions of UK aircraft journals fall into this category. Most trade magazines fall somewhere between the two.

Publishers would have us believe that a special show edition, full of ads, advertorial and puffery, is for the benefit of their readers who require a foretaste of what's in store. The truth is that the motivation is more likely to be a prime opportunity to extract extra revenue from their long-suffering advertisers. I don't believe that many readers do what the publishers would have you believe and take the journal to use as the primary exhibition guide. It's much easier to get the official one at the door.

Well, will you swallow that tempting offer? Even in the worst case, it probably is worth including the show edition in your normal schedule. There will possibly be a longer print run and readers do tend to keep copies longer, but whether they use them as standard reference works on a daily basis is debatable.

On the other hand, if there is editorial offered to advertisers, and you can get a decent chunk of the page to yourself and a couple of photographs, this may be worth having, especially if you want to break some great company news.

When the space-buying decision has been mine, I have normally resisted the temptation, mainly because it creates a precedent. Buy unscheduled space just once, and you will be hounded constantly by space salespeople.

If, however, you have included the show edition in your schedule, you can tailor your standard ad to suit the occasion. Most companies realise that it is worth adding a small flash to their press ads to promote their presence at a trade show. Apart from a minor alteration to the artwork, it costs nothing.

■ Public Relations

PR is a different matter entirely. Another person who suddenly becomes very friendly is the 'suit' from your PR agency, who sniffs rich pickings as surely as a hyena following a pride of lions.

'Hi, Tarquin here. Componex time again. Fancy a bite at the Fox and Hounds?'

Why not? You know there is no such thing as a free lunch, but this one might be a reasonable investment. Your PR agency can be great value for money. Choose one that specialises in your line of business. PR agencies are not bound, as ad agencies are, by rules that prevent them from handling competitive accounts. A specialist agency will have a grasp of the technical aspects and the culture and conventions of your industry. They also will have long-established media contacts and be able to place stories.

■ Time consciousness

Be warned, however. You will probably be billed for every hour devoted to your business, even if you have a consultancy agreement. And hours mount up very quickly, especially when spent quaffing Cointreaus after a heavy lunch. I set a ceiling on spending. When the money's gone, it's gone.

■ Show time is news time

Show time is when every exhibitor tries to get the maximum media coverage. This is when your PR agency will show their mettle. Stories don't just have to be concerned with the new products to be launched at Componex. They can introduce newly joined executives, sponsorship deals, a new website or customer care initiative. And with every company story that appears, in whatever context, take the opportunity to mention your presence at the show and the number of your stand.

■ The flowing of creative juices

There is another caveat when dealing with the PR agency. Ever hopeful of 'adding value', they will come up with a whole raft of wacky ideas. Some are thrown in to the melting pot just to impress you on their creative ability. Only accept ideas that you know are within their capability and whose costs can be controlled. When the creative juices flow, so does the cash.

Many times I have heard highly original ideas from agency people presented with tremendous enthusiasm and conviction. When they draw breathlessly to a close, I ask, 'What will it cost?' 'We're working on that now,' they reply. You'll have the answer shortly.'

■ The Law of PR returns

I read between the lines. This is their code for 'We've had this weirdo pop in with a really crazy idea which we would like to get into our portfolio to show how creative we are. We're looking for somebody to try it out for us and you seem just the person.' The reason they can't give you a price is that they are chasing that creative genius for a figure, but can't get one calculated until he comes round from the latest binge of booze and dope.

Believe me, assume that highly original agency ideas are expensive until proved otherwise. The irrefutable law of PR returns states that the cost is always greater than the originality of the idea, but it is probably worth paying in the long term. Looked at another way, creative ideas are what marks you out from the crowd. You choose.

Chapter 13

Getting There and Getting In

■ Transport – To Site and On Site

Just getting to the venue can produce drama by itself. You know how difficult it is going on holiday. All that paperwork. The hassle with airlines. All the last-minute things you need to buy. Then to satisfy the most personal needs, there is rarely enough room in your suitcase.

■ Taking a small house

Now you are doing much the same, only taking the equivalent of a small house, which needs erecting in two days and taking apart in one. If when you go on holiday you leave your sponge bag behind, it's no big deal. You buy another one. When you are exhibiting, anything you leave behind normally has to be fetched or sent on. If it is sourced locally, the supplier knows you are desperate and will overcharge accordingly.

■ Going abroad

Normally a stand builder will have all the experience necessary to get your stand to the venue. He will have done it more times than he has had lukewarm Costa coffee. Luckily he will know all about carnets and other baffling procedures. However, if you send him to far-flung places, he may not be quite so conversant with national regulations and customs. He will probably be aware which countries prohibit heavy goods vehicle movement on Sundays, but there are bound to be things that catch him out. My only advice is not to cut any timings too fine. Half a day lost at a border checkpoint could mean more than half a day lost at the venue, because many shows have timetables for unloading and woe betide any driver who misses his slot. So never complain at the bill for an extra night at a trucky's flop which seems unjustified.

■ Space on the truck

Luckily the stand contractor undertakes to transport everything structural for you and will, for the price of a pint, bung in much besides. Most contractors have spare space in their trucks after the stand is loaded, so it makes sense to send print, samples and graphics with them if you can. You do have to remember that your stuff is there on sufferance. It's always best to load it first if you can, on the principle of first on, last off. If it's in the way when the chippies unload, they are quite likely to leave it standing in the rain while they get their stuff unloaded.

There will also be suppliers delivering things independently. Make sure they have full instructions on how to get to the convention centre, with a map, your stand number and, most of important of all, your mobile phone number.

■ DIY transportation

If you have booked a shell stand space, however, you will probably be taking the lot yourself in your own or hired vehicle. So the first rule is . . . MAKE AN INVENTORY.

List everything you need. In addition to the bigger items, like graphics panels, I always take a laptop, a concertina filing box for all the documentation, and a self-preservation kit. The self-preservation kit includes all those little things that you need in a hurry, especially when the shops are shut. These are what I put in mine:

- Scissors
- Tacking/stapling gun
- Spirit level

- Tape measure
- Ruler
- Paper stapler
- Hook and loop tape and tabs
- Gaffer tape
- Various adhesives (Superglue, PVA glue and a heat glue gun)
- Small self-charging drill and screwdriver
- Box of screws
- Box of drawing pins
- Notepad and pens
- Envelopes
- Minidisk recorder and disks
- Digital camera
- Calculator
- Post-it pads
- Large felt-tip markers
- Business cards
- Small torch

If you take power tools, take cheap ones. Anything expensive will walk. (Cheap ones often do as well, but the loss isn't so great.) Paint your name on them, so that if there is a dispute, ownership isn't in question. If yours is a common name add an initial to be on the safe side.

Arrival at the venue

Arriving at a venue and starting work always leaves me with mixed emotions. Large convention centres are daunting, with their gaping hangar doors, dour and unhelpful staff and unbelievably complex car park arrangements. Even the impressive 'exhibitor' sticker on your windscreen doesn't cut any ice. Nobody here seems to have heard of the customer being king. Exhibitors seem to be the lowest form of crawling life.

Getting exhibits to the hall isn't always as easy as it seems (Photo courtesy of Project Profile)

■ The Build

Nevertheless, you go in search of your stand site. Inside the hall, it is one gigantic construction site, with stands in all stages of completion. I understand how Howard Hughes must have felt when he turned up each morning to review the progress in building the 'Spruce Goose'. Somehow, even though you know the hall plan backwards, the stand is never quite where you imagine it to be.

Progress is never as far advanced as on everyone else's stand. I seem always to find that our stand is way behind. While other builders are wielding paintbrushes, mine are still at the Black & Decker stage. I have learnt not to be fazed. I have confidence that the builders know their business, and I am rarely let down. Together we have reached that wonderful degree of trust where I trust them not to forget than one vital component and they trust me not to make more than one important change of mind at the last moment. It seems to work.

■ **Why be there?**

Although you may not have anything physical to do while the builders are beavering away, you should be there during all but the early stages of the build. You feel awkward standing around without an apparent purpose while everybody else knows exactly what to do. What seems to make it worse is they have always seen you before in a suit and here you are in sweatshirt and jeans. The normal business relationship of client and supplier changes. You are now part of one team.

There are good reasons to be there. Decisions have to be made on the fly, as problems arise. You may spot flaws in the design that weren't apparent from the plan. The sooner they are rectified the better. Typical are cupboard doors that don't open because a shelf is in the way, or a demonstration machine needs room for a collecting tray that wasn't mentioned at the planning stage.

■ **Your place in the village**

On that very first day on site, there is inevitably a thrill in seeing something that has been no more than a few lines on a plan or an artist's impression, becoming a reality. It assumes shape and scale. Whereas on the plan you always regarded it in isolation, it now becomes part of a neighbourhood of stands. Part of a small village, where neighbours are already becoming acquaintances and drinking buddies.

This is the time you discover how well your stand stacks up against its competitors. Walk along the aisles, approaching the stand from each direction. View it critically. Although it is too late to overcome major shortcomings, there may yet be ways of tweaking to overcome minor problems, like sightlines to monitors, positioning of logos and improving access.

Most important of all, you are learning about the stand and how it operates. So if there is a power problem during the show, you will be able to track it to its source because you watched the electrician installing the cables and junction boxes. Invariably they won't be as marked on the plan.

Being around during the build allows you to plan how you will operate it. You will see for the first time just how much room there is.

■ The danger in being too advanced

Danger lurks for those who are ready too soon. The company bigwigs and ad agency people come down a couple of days before opening, and they invariably want changes to be made. Tarquin has been exercising his creative muscles again.

'I've had this great idea,' he says. 'It came to me in bed last night. If you move that upright six inches to the right, you could install a bubblegum machine.'

'A bubblegum machine? What on earth for?'

'Simple. The average piece of gum lasts 20 minutes. So when they leave your stand, they will still be chewing on your gum. Your proposition will be with them until the flavour runs out and they dump the gum. And we've got a slogan as well.'

'Go on, Tarquin, dazzle me.'

'We have the solution to your needs. Hear us out and chew it over.'

'Sorry, Tarquin.' But you don't want to discourage the creative genius, even if you think his rationale a smidgeon flawed. 'It's a great idea, but not great enough to justify a major reconstruction.'

'Pity. Jason thinks it is.'

'Really, Tark. You might have asked me first.'

'But you weren't around, old boy. Down here with the workers.' He makes it sound as if I am at a coalface in Durham.

Space is, of course, measured up for a bubblegum machine at vast inconvenience and with much head scratching. It will put back the construction by at least four hours. Then you are struck by one of those Eureka! moments. You find Tarquin reconnoitring the dark storeroom assigned for the Press Office.

'Tarquin, terribly sorry,' you lie, 'but the organisers have a by-law against chewing gum in Hall 5. It used to cost them a thousand pounds a year to have it scraped off the floors.'

'Oh, you're kidding! But you've got to agree it was a stroke of genius.'

'It certainly was, Tark, old chap. One of your best.'

You give a sigh of relief as another crisis was avoided by fast thinking and diplomacy.

■ Allow For Things To Go Wrong – They Will!

I'm sure you don't want a list of disasters that have beset me and my friends. Many are too painful to relate. What I have learnt is that you can mitigate against them.

Here are some basic defences against Murphy's Law:

- Allow more time than you need. I suggest a third more.
- Build a small contingency into your budget, and don't spend it until you absolutely have to. Some public sector clients won't recognise contingencies, so you'll have to call them something else.
- Assign responsibilities so that if anything does go wrong you will not be alone in sorting it out.
- Delegate current work so that you can concentrate on what's coming up. More easily said than done.
- Have somebody back at base who is fully briefed, so that anything left behind or replacements can be sent on.
- Carry reserves of anything likely to breakdown or fail.

They are probably unrealistic, but worth a try.

■ Pre-opening Audit and Technical Check – Does It All Work?

There you are on the night before the show. You're bone tired, aching in every joint and dying for a drink. This is the time when real professionalism shows. Ignore the pleas to go to the bar. Get out your list and check everything. Don't tick off anything unless you are satisfied you have an answer.

Here's a checklist I use:

- The structure. Is it complete, robust and safe?
- Decorating. Is painting finished? Do all finishes match? Is there any wet paint that needs warning signs?
- Doors and lockers. Do they shut and lock?
- Check for pockets of planings and wood chippings that could be a fire hazard.
- Electric points. Is there power at each one?
- Electric cables. Are they hidden? Are there any loose ends that need gaffer-taping until a more permanent solution can be devised?
- Telephone connections. Are they live? Are they labelled?
- Carpets. Are they tacked down everywhere?
- Furniture. Do you have everything you ordered? Is the colour right?
- Lights. Do they all work? Where are the spare lamps?
- PCs, laptops and similar gadgets. Are they locked away or adequately fixed?
- Graphics. Give each one a last-minute check for spellings. There might just be time to get corrections done. Are they securely fixed?
- Demonstrations. Does demo equipment work? Is the auditorium safe, with adequate access, disability ramps and good sight lines?
- Do you have an emergency repair kit for mechanical and electrical repairs, and a first aid kit?
- Leaflet dispensers. Are they securely fixed and loaded?
- Print and giveaways. Do you have enough for the first day?
- Noticeboard. Is there a noticeboard? And are stand regulations, rotas and timetables accessible for stand staff?

You don't have to be 100 per cent ready. But you do need to know what has to be done. Some jobs will have to be completed before leaving, some can wait until you arrive in the morning and some can even wait for a convenient break.

What To Do If You're Not Ready On Time

The time will inevitably come in your exhibiting career when the gods of exhibition decide that you have in some way offended them. Their vengeance will be wrought in many ways, the most daunting being that they prevent your stand being completed by the time the show opens.

You will feel devastated. It's all highly embarrassing and no doubt the Argonaut will be arriving soon after opening to receive his fair share of the glory.

■ Keeping your cool

What do you do? You soldier on, ignoring the taunts of your neighbours and competitors. What you do *not* do is panic. If the crisis is a major one, get your team together and work out a solution with them. You will find (in most cases) that the stand builders are a tower of strength when it comes to matters structural. They have seen it all before and they'll find a answer quicker than you would think possible. It usually involves a quick trip to the nearest builders' merchants and a lot of banging.

In my experience, most such problems result from deliveries not arriving on time or being sent to the wrong place. And in many cases the fault lies with you for not giving clear enough instructions or allowing them sufficient time.

If you are really in the deep and smelly, and the stand is an absolute mess, cut your losses. Close the stand and hire a meeting room until it is sorted out. In the worst scenario, visitors would have to dodge workmen with electrical tools and tins of paint. You can't do business under these conditions. And it is almost certain that any accidents resulting will not be covered by your public liability. If the convention centre can't help, find a nearby hotel.

Chapter 14

Stand Management

■ Rules of Engagement and Selling Techniques

'Come off it. Three days away from the family. Fancy hotel. Good clubbing. It'll be well cool.'

Many otherwise normal employees view exhibitions as an excuse for escaping the constraints of their normal business life and families. 'Free,' they claim, 'but for a few hours of chatting to customers and prospects.' They are wrong. They may be free of the day-to-day drudgery of routine selling, but the time should be replaced by a regime every bit as ordered and tightly controlled. Exhibitions are not about wild assaults on the city's all-night discos or seedy shebeens. Being unfit for work or slovenly on the stand is a mortal sin.

Make sure everyone understands from the outset that exhibiting is sheer bloody hard work. To the eight hours each day on the stand will be added several more in reviewing progress, consolidating business and planning the next day. To ensure that all the work is done there have to be rules, rotas and responsibilities.

■ Rotas

'It's like you're making us go back to school!'

Yes, it's exactly like going back to school. Many staff, on arrival at the exhibition venue, seem to revert to being unruly kids. Normally sensible Bill Brown and Sharon Green become fifth-form dropouts when away from home. Everybody should know when they are on and off duty and what their extra tasks for the day are. In addition to getting the work done, it demonstrates to all that you are being fair.

■ Fun

Emphasise that although exhibiting is hard work, it is also rewarding and can be fun. Try to build in fun features, especially those that stimulate competitive spirit.

■ Relationships

One interpretation of fun you can do without is what might be loosely termed 'relationships'. The heady mixture of hotel-living and copious quantities of alcohol is bound to generate 'one night stands', but they should never be allowed to go further. The problem is that with all your other urgent tasks, you will be the last to find out about affairs and by then it will be too late.

Nip it in the bud before you even leave for the exhibition. Inform your staff that anybody spending the night in somebody else's hotel room will be immediately sent home and a report sent to the Argonaut. Of course, they know that he will just chuckle and file it away, because he too may have been up to mischief, and they also know that who slept where is impossible to prove. Nevertheless, it is worth making the point before they have had time to exchange knowing winks.

■ Briefing and Training

'Come off it. You don't need to teach me anything about selling. Every bone in my body is a selling bone.'

Of course they don't like being told. They've been plodding round their territory for years. You have to inform them tactfully that this is different, and success will depend on their preparation for the task ahead.

■ Brief before the show

If at all possible, brief your stand staff before you leave for the show. If you can also get them together for a day's training, so much the better. If you can't arrange anything back at the office, book a room at your hotel the evening before the show opens.

We've all seen it at exhibitions, haven't we? I call it the 'Hotel Reception' approach. Salespeople arrive fresh from the car park, taxi rank and train station, suitcases in hand at their stand on opening morning as if they were booking into a hotel, coats over their arms, overnight bags on trolleys and laptops on shoulder. They are then given a five-minute pep talk by the stand manager and expected to get to work immediately. The poor, bemused individuals are more interested in where to put their things and getting a cup of decent coffee. How can they possibly perform efficiently?

Here are some suggestions for the briefing session:

- **Objectives.**
  The objectives for exhibiting should be made clear at the outset. In addition to overall objectives, allocate daily quotas to keep the staff on their toes. You might even have a competition with a worthwhile incentive.
- **Stand layout.**
  Everybody should know where everything is, how to open up in the morning and close down at night.
- **Responsibilities and duties.**
  Spread the responsibilities liberally. The stand manager is a very overworked person, so the more duties that can be delegated the better. Staff should also know who to contact when a need arises. I always have a contact list in the stand log and pinned up in a cupboard together with a complete list of mobile phone numbers.
- **Logistics.**
  Make sure they know how to get to their hotels, what they are expected to bring and the timings. You will have little time to sort out problems on site.

Training is important

I have mentioned the importance of pre-show briefing. Pre-show training is just as important.

The old way

There's a principle of industrial training that goes back to ancient times, called 'sitting with Nellie'. The callow stripling is assigned to an ancient sage, normally somebody who has long since abandoned any ambition or wish to innovate, and the new employee learns by watching and asking. They also learn all the short cuts and the sharp practices, and cynicism towards management. The loveable old-timer who has done it for donkeys' years is rarely the best mentor.

Yet that is the principle of much on-stand training. Young sales people are assigned to old Dennis, a 60-year-old veteran of 20 Componexes. Not a good idea. Old Dennis will probably need training as much as all the rest, maybe more.

Off-site training

If you are really serious about exhibiting, you must train all the staff you are likely to use on the stand. We all know it's difficult to get a sales force off the road for a day. They will try every excuse in the book and then invent some new ones. Added to that you will have field sales managers, national accounts managers and managers from departments you've never even heard of on your back. Just stick to your guns and explain the importance of the session. If there is a cost, you might have to bear it.

Contracted staff

It's also expensive to bring in contracted hospitality staff for training, but it is worth doing. Maybe the agency will let them come for a reduced fee for a non-operational day. The other difficulty with agencies is that they like swapping staff about at the last minute, so you must insist that the people who come to your training session are the same ones who will be there for the show. You don't believe an agency would be so stupid as to send different people even after you have expressly trained them? Think again!

The value of off-site training is that while it needs to be structured, it can be relatively informal and proceed at the pace of the trainees. If they don't grasp a particular point, you can pause and explain or practise it.

A typical programme

A day's training programme should be a blend of instruction and practical exercises. Treat it like a serious training day, with a proper programme and a full set of training aids. Invest an afternoon's time putting together a PowerPoint presentation for them. It does mean a lot of work for you, probably when you are under the greatest pressure, but it's well worth it. I like to divide the day into a theory morning and a practical afternoon.

Mobile phones

When your trainees arrive, confiscate all mobile phones. Switching off is insufficient, as your class will be constantly taking comfort breaks to call from the cloakroom.

Simulate the stand environment

Book a large room, if possible one that is as large as your stand, and mark out on the floor where the walls and various elements will be with gaffer tape, so that the class will have some concept of the scale of the structure. In the afternoon, simulate reception desks with tables and put chairs where your chat area will be.

Some companies own their own sets of Marler-Hayley or similar display panels. During the lunch break, you could erect these to represent walls and structural features so that they become solid obstacles. The more realistic you make it, the better. The class can then practise their approach to prospects and so on.

■ Video, the great deflater

Using a video camera can also be useful. When shown on a monitor, faults and technique problems become obvious and everybody benefits. It is strange how a class that claimed to know everything there is to know about selling will quickly become subdued and realise just how limited and clumsy their techniques really are, especially when confronted by space and time constraints. There is no greater deflator of egos than a video camera.

■ Programme

Here is a typical programme for a one day training course:

9.30	Assemble, coffee and look at model or visuals of stand
9.45	Presentation – Objectives of the exhibition
10.00	Presentation – The role of the exhibition in selling and marketing
10.15	Presentation – The stand layout and how it works
10.30	Presentation – Stand management
10.45	Discussion
11.15	Break
11.45	Handling prospects
	Follow-up and post-exhibition activity
12.30	Lunch
13.15	Role-playing, practical exercises and discussion
15.30	Tea and adjourn

■ Brought-in training aids – 'Can I help you?'

There are training videos on the market covering many aspects of exhibiting. Should you use them? That depends really on your presentational skills. Except in very large companies, the size of the class will be quite small, so running the sessions should not be too intimidating. Use only outside training aids that fit your plan. Never adapt your ideas to somebody else's theories if you don't believe them. I certainly wouldn't expect you to follow the advice I give in this book if you think it a load of tosh.

One video on exhibiting really annoys me. I don't know if it is still being used, but it made a big impact for many years. A major point made in it was that on a stand nobody should ever approach a mildly interested prospect with the question, 'Can I help you?' The premise was that it invited the answer, 'No!' End of conversation. Instead, you should ask something like, 'We have a brand new widget. Can I show you?' Dialogue is established. It all sounds so logical, doesn't it? Until you return to the basics of salesmanship. We are actually there to help our customers, not to ram down their throats products that they don't want.

Another basic principle of selling is to ask questions and build a picture of your contact's needs. If you open by explaining for five minutes about the advances of the Mark 2 Widget over the Mark 1, your visitor will listen politely and wander off when you have finished, clutching your brochure and a free pen. If the prospect isn't in the market for either the Mark 1 or the Mark 2, you have not only wasted valuable time, but you have probably missed an opportunity elsewhere.

■ 'Can I help you?' is correct

So in fact, the sentiment behind 'Can I help you?' is absolutely correct. That is what people want to hear. Not some carefully rehearsed sales patter about the new widget. You need to engage your prospect or customer. The only way you will achieve that is by opening on their business, not yours. Possibly there are better ways of asking the question. Maybe something like, 'What business are you in?' Then listen to the reply and come back with something like, 'So you have pretty impressive plans for expansion, then?'

Perhaps the producers of that video lived in that happy era of sellers' markets – if it ever really existed. Today, most companies are selling in crowded market places and in many, the products or services are reduced to almost commodity status. Added value is everything.

We will examine the principles of selling on an exhibition stand in some detail in Chapter 16.

■ Safety Issues Before Opening

Whether we like it or not, health and safety issues rule our lives. At an exhibition, somebody has to be responsible and the chances are that it will be the stand manager.

In my experience, you can never cover every eventuality. If you did, the stand would be impossible to work. So you do the best you can. I will come on to the major issues of health and safety as a separate topic, but for now let's look at safety issues you should impress on staff before the show starts.

- Nobody should be allowed on a stand under construction without the manager's permission and certainly should not help the construction crew.
- Nobody, but nobody, must repair any electrical fault at any time. Of course, they will. Human nature being what it is, some DIY dab hand among your staff will mend a poor connection with a bit of insulation tape. But warn them that tampering with electrics will be a disciplinary offence.
- On double-deck stands under construction, nobody may be on the stand without a hard hat. Nor should anybody climb to more than 2.4m off the ground unless they have been on a formal safety course.

■ A Uniform Approach

■ I haven't got anything to wear

Not only is this cry of despair heard on receiving a wedding invitation, it also appears to cause much dispute before an exhibition. Everybody has a view on what stand staff should wear.

It really all comes back to branding and image. Corporate culture will no doubt be a major determining factor. Generally speaking you should be dressed in a way that makes it easy to interact with visitors. Although few visitors go to exhibitions in suits, preferring something more comfortable for a long day on their feet, they do try to look reasonably smart at many business-to-business shows.

So it is only right that you too should look smart and restrained. If suits are the order of the day, they must look immaculate and freshly pressed.

◼ Suits you, sir

It is also good to consider what people feel happiest working in. Some salespeople only seem to feel comfortable in suits. They apparently need the authority and the image of professionalism that more formal dress imparts. Others are more comfortable in polo shirts. Unfortunately, for the sake of uniformity, individual tastes cannot be indulged.

If suits are worn, corporate ties or lapel badges help visitors identify your staff. Alternatively, wear red carnations. Anything that is immediately recognisable.

Suits are fine on a restrained, conservative stand, but they can look totally out of place on a more adventurous creation where the company is trying in every way to generate a cool image. Polo shirts or even T-shirts with appropriate slogans or motifs are an immediate signal of informality. When visitors come to see you, they expect fun. You could even go one better and dress your staff in boiler suits. Everyone will then know you mean business.

I mentioned earlier a stand that had been constructed to look like a tropical beach. The two guys running it dressed in character, with loud shirts and Bermuda shorts. Not only did they stand out from the ubiquitous grey suits, but they looked as if they were enjoying every minute of it.

With contract staff, a smart uniform is the order of the day. It doesn't have to look as if it's been issued to British Airways flight attendants. A trip to Marks & Spencer or Next can produce something attractive that will suit everybody and be available in a range of sizes.

Chapter 15

Health and Safety

Now there's an emotive phrase. Three words guaranteed to raise a groan. To most of us it smacks of 'jobsworth' and bureaucracy. Nevertheless, it is something that you have to take seriously in exhibiting. You are dealing with hazardous materials like pieces of four by two timber and sharp implements like Stanley knives. Coping with the increasingly safety-conscious world and the vast amount of paperwork that goes with it is one of the most arduous and often meaningless aspects of exhibition work. While I do appreciate that building temporary structures at breakneck speed does have risks, the task is normally carried out by proficient people.

■ A mass of regulations

When you look through your exhibitor's handbook, you will be amazed at the number and detail of the constraints you have to abide by. The first level is imposed by the law of the land, with the guiding legislation being the Health and Safety at Work Act 1974. On top of this are regulations, codes of practice and directives from a variety of sources. If you exhibiting out of doors, there will be local by-laws.

Moses would have had a field day with all of these: 'If thou requirest a gas-fired cooker, thou shalt employ a CORGI registered engineer.' 'Thou art entrusted to use only construction materials which have been tested in accordance with BS 476.' The venue then adds a few of their own: 'Thou shalt not construct a structure above 4.2 metres in height.' And so it goes on . . . and on. If you are an insomniac, take the organiser's 'Guide for Exhibitors' to bed with you.

■ Can you chance it?

So do you have to obey them all? The simple answer is yes, and as with everything else connected with matters legal, ignorance is no defence. In practice it isn't always easy. I suppose I shouldn't write this down in case I incriminate myself, but, yes, I have taken a chance from time to time. Naturally I can't condone such things in print. If you do so, it's the unwritten rule that you must obey: 'Thou shalt not be caught out.' It's when things go wrong that the questions are asked, and then that you'd better have the answers. In the meantime, many of us suffer from whatever condition it is that results from permanently crossed fingers.

Health and safety has its own set of carved tablets. Of course, you as an employer are only too aware of that new breed of lawyers who are just waiting to drag you into the courts. Exhibitions are full of hazards during build and strike. Everyone is in a rush to complete on time and there is a great temptation to cut corners when things get behind schedule. Don't be tempted to meet the deadline at any cost. If somebody gets hurt, the cost will be too great.

However, enough moralising. It is just something we have to live with. We must smile sweetly at the officious man with a clipboard, we must study the small print and we must wear our hard hats even when the heaviest things that can fall on us are made of polystyrene.

I would commend to you an excellent publication that costs you absolutely nothing. It is called 'The Big Red Book' and can be downloaded from website of the Association of Exhibition Organisers (www.aeo.org.uk). The link is: http://www.aeo.org.uk/page.cfm/Link=40/t=m/goSection=7

■ A duty of care

Nevertheless we do have a duty of care to the general public and our staff. And we should never presume upon their common sense. There are hordes of hungry lawyers out there waiting for the moment when somebody trips on your carpet or scratches themselves on a loose piece of trim. If the level of safety required goes way beyond what seems logical there is frequently a good reason. Somewhere, somebody has been the victim of litigation and has had to pay a small fortune for a sprained ankle or bump on the head.

The biggest problem I have with safety is time. Time for meetings. Time for tests on materials. And time taken in filling in forms. In your planning, you just have to allow adequate time for it all.

■ Safety Officer

Every stand must have a safety officer. Since nobody in their right mind will take on the task, it might as well be you. At least you will know the job is being done well, or if not you can have the excuses ready.

Having reluctantly awarded yourself the privileged post, what are your duties?

- To acquaint yourself with all the regulations. These are not just those contained in the exhibition pack. If you are abroad, you may be subject to all sorts of unfamiliar laws and the only way to learn about them is from somebody local. Chambers of Commerce are very helpful here and so is the Department of Trade and Industry.
- To ensure that you or the contractors have all the relevant documentation. This will cover fire certificates, material specifications and even certificates of competence for specialist staff. If you can, compile a folder containing them all and if you can't get the originals, use copies. A thick wad of official-looking documents produced instantly has been known to defuse a nasty situation instantly.
- To check that all your staff who are required to undertake any physical task have the relevant competence to do so, both in skill and fitness terms. You think this is unlikely to be a major concern? You won't be asking your staff to be doing anything dangerous, will you? One of the most frequent health and safety issues is back injury from lifting heavy weights. Stacks of print are exceedingly heavy and difficult to grip. For somebody unused to lifting or with an old injury, there is always a risk.

- To maintain a first aid kit. It is not enough to place it on the stand at the start of the show. It must be inspected regularly. You will find that sticking plasters are taken to hold up display boards and the asprin supply soon becomes depleted with so many hangovers to cure.
- To check with your insurance company that the company's public liability insurance covers your exhibition activities. If it doesn't, correct the situation immediately.

■ Risk Assessments

Now here's an emotive subject. How risky is the average shell stand? Roughly comparable to inviting some friends into your living room. Nothing dangerous in that, is there? The powers that be see even that as a hazardous pursuit. Chelmsford Borough Council issues guidelines on writing risk assessments in one of their events packs and give as an example the holding of a coffee morning. Before reading these alarming revelations I never realised that little old ladies holding such seemingly innocuous events for the benefit of the local church were really facing great danger.

The principle of the risk assessment is that you identify every possible eventuality that might harm either your staff or the general public. You then assess the relative risk and probability of the worst outcome happening. Then you explain what measures you have taken or will take to protect everyone against that happening. Does that make sense? Probably not. I suppose the justification for risk analyses is that they make you think about potential hazards.

If you are puzzled, there are plenty of websites with sample forms. Pick one that seems most appropriate and change it to fit your need.

■ Insurance

For an activity so vulnerable to human frailty and the unpredictable as exhibiting, you must take insurance seriously. Yet Insurex Expo-Sure, one of the leading specialist event and exhibition insurance suppliers, claims that only 10 per cent of companies arrange suitable or adequate cover. But then, their view of what is adequate cover may differ from yours, especially when you get their quote. Whether you take their advice or not, it is worth listening to.

It is true to say that you can insure against almost any eventuality at a price. Here are some that are often quoted:

- Cancellation or closure of the event, resulting in unrecoverable costs.
- Transportation delays and breakdowns.
- Damage to stand and equipment in transit and erection.
- Losses at the exhibition itself due to theft or mishandling.
- Travel insurance for staff attending the show.

You can even insure against the anticipated numbers of visitors failing to turn up due to some external reason, like a natural disaster.

Some show organisers offer insurance schemes for exhibitors at their shows and, because the volume of business is likely to be great, they are usually good value.

What sort of policy you take out depends very much on the scale of your exhibiting. If you are attending only a couple of major shows a year, you can take out policies for individual events, or you can have an annual policy based on your schedule of events.

You would also be well advised to make sure that your cover includes all expensive equipment like computers, monitors and projectors. Neither should you neglect to insure anything you hire. Sometimes a hire company will require evidence that their equipment will be covered before they will deliver.

■ Legal obligations

Your company must have employers' liability insurance and the chances are it will also have public liability insurance. So you have every right to assume that your stand, its staff and the general public will be covered along with everything else, don't you?

■ Don't assume anything

Unfortunately, this may not be so. So pop along to the company secretary and ask their advice. You may find that cover applies only to company premises. You might consider the stand as being part of those premises, but the insurance company will be doubtful. And when they are doubtful, they don't pay.

Often it is both more convenient and cheaper to include employers' and public liability in your exhibiting policy. The public liability cover will normally be £5 million and that should be sufficient for most eventualities.

I have learnt from experience that Sod's Law works with a vengeance where insurance is concerned. It strikes those who are under-insured hardest. If you have adequate cover, you will probably never need it and resent having to pay the premiums. But at least you'll sleep at nights.

■ Security

Despite the most stringent precautions, you will lose things. There is nothing like an exhibition to encourage inanimate objects to sprout legs and run. It does not matter how exalted the visitor profile, how big the item or how tightly it is screwed down. I remember a launch by Apple of a new range of computers to its dealer principals. A computer disappeared almost from under the noses of Apple staff and the chances are that it was taken by one of the dealers. Lengths of Trilite, hefty three-sided trussing, have been lifted while waiting to be carted from truck to stand site. And curiously framed pictures of little value to anybody outside the owner's company have been unscrewed and removed. The light-fingered have inherited the world, or at least the exhibition world.

I apologise if all this is causing you to have second thoughts about exhibiting in Moscow or Dubai. The rewards still far outweigh the risk. Provided you take reasonable precautions, your losses should be within manageable proportions.

■ Making Certain that Things Don't Walk During the Night

■ Remove anything portable when the stand is unoccupied

Whether you hire venue security or not, at night take away anything portable that is valuable. Laptops are the easiest to steal and so are most attractive to thieves. Everything of yours at risk on the stand should be marked with an identification mark. It will be difficult to reclaim anything if it isn't. This is even more true abroad. If you want start an international incident, try asking a local security officer to stop a man you think has absconded with your mobile phone.

Mind you, having said that, I have taken things back to the hotel, only to have them stolen from my room.

■ Lockable areas

Wherever you go and no matter how small the stand, have a space that can be locked up. It probably won't be much of a hindrance to a determined thief, but it will deter the opportunist.

Any valuable equipment that has to remain overnight should be secured to the stand structure. Clearly, removal is not possible with built-in DVD players and hardwired PCs. Access panels for such equipment are often only too obvious, so try and make them harder to find and open without the thief causing suspicious behaviour. Put wire strops onto the equipment as a deterrent. While it's easy to break a lock, freeing a strop requires disturbing the stand structure or walking around with a pair of hefty bolt-croppers. Neither are low profile options favoured by petty crooks.

■ Take the key out

If a cupboard contains anything valuable, keep it locked and put the key in your pocket. An interesting diversion at any large show is to walk around and observe how many secure-looking cupboards on stands have keys left in the locks. And, of course, you may not be alone in the pastime.

Don't believe that, because there is somebody on duty, everything is safe. Thieves work in teams. While one distracts the salesperson with a tempting enquiry, the other goes in search of briefcases, handbags, laptops and mobile phones. It is so easy. And once snatched, they will have a plan for the rapid disposal of the snatched goods. So even though they are spotted making a getaway, retrieving anything is unlikely.

■ Out of harm's way

Where you place your cupboard also has a bearing on its security. In a room separate from the main stand area is ideal, but even on the open plan stand some options are better than others. Put yourself in the mindset of the thief and think of ways that would make them think twice before making a snatch:

- Reception desk. If the desk is permanently manned, then having the cupboard under the counter is relatively secure.
- Don't make it too obvious. A six-foot door always conceals a coat rack and where you leave your coat is normally where you leave your briefcase. Thieves know this. Avoid making the door look like a cupboard door. Too often it is surrounded with a wooden moulding or painted in a different colour. I have even seen cupboards with signs saying 'storeroom'. Instead disguise it as a display panel or part of your corporate décor.
- An unusual place. Thieves will always look in the obvious places first. If you place it at ground level under a desk or use the space beneath your bench seating, anybody trying to gain access immediately looks suspicious.

■ Patrols

Large shows have roving patrols outside show hours. Their function is general security and not to keep an eye on your stand unless you pay them to do so. There is always the suspicion that this is some form of protection racket. It isn't normally, at least not in the UK.

If you want patrols to watch your stand, you have to pay for the service. They will then pop in on their round and check it for you. I'm not sure quite how effective this is. It is certainly useful to have somebody making sure that you've locked everything up or not left a screen on. But standing patrols are too predictable to deter anyone seriously bent on mischief. I also often wonder who walks abroad in the dead of night pinching the toffees and pocketing the free ballpoints. Nobody ever catches them at it.

■ Full-time security staff

Sometimes you need to have full-time security on your stand. If you have anything valuable on show, your insurance company may insist. Professionals are best left to do the job themselves. However, you might have to brief them yourself. Security falls into two categories:

- Deterrence.
  This is where the security team are dressed in uniform. Their purpose is to deter those with evil intent from attempting anything.
- Surveillance.
  Here the team try to remain unobtrusive, and try to catch perpetrators red-handed. They are better positioned off the stand, where they can watch visitors approaching and leaving, without attracting attention to themselves.

■ Sabotage

Vicious sabotage is rare. On the other hand, jolly japes by your competitors may not be. There is something about a trade fair that brings to the surface latent remnants of school days in many people – those who can't see a high structure without experiencing an insatiable urge to hang a pair of knickers on it. They can't view a picture of your company chairman without wanting to add a moustache and pipe in felt-tip. And they can't resist adding a letter on a display to turn an innocuous word into something offensive. All a bit of fun, they think. Not to the poor sod who has to put it right.

The problem with this type of sabotage is that it is difficult to stop. The perpetrators may be friends who have the same access to the hall as yourself. They may know when your staff are occupied with a photo call. And the tools of their trade are simple, innocent and easy to conceal. Unfortunately they also know the risk of being caught is small.

■ The T-word

As if thieving weren't bad enough, we now have to consider the threats of international terrorism, smuggling and international crime that have settled on the modern world. I doubt if they will affect you if all you have is a small shell stand in the UK.

On the other hand, once you embark on an international programme of events, you are bound to run into one or other of these nasties. The frightening aspect of it all is that if you fall victim, you will discover you have few friends. Insurance companies will point to the exclusion clauses in the small print. Local police are often unsympathetic and may not have officers who speak English. And British consuls and embassy staff seem powerless.

■ Smuggling

In the case of smuggling, where your truck has, without your knowledge, become the hiding place for a stash of drugs, you may even be judged guilty and have to prove your innocence. Many an innocent exhibitor has become entangled in international crime without the slightest suspicion that they are being targeted. The only defence is vigilance. Inspect your flight cases before you seal them. When you load the truck, always have a reliable person keeping watch. Then seal the truck tight.

Chapter 16

Working the Stand

On that first day of the show you step aboard, like the captain of a destroyer about to leave port and do battle with an enemy way beyond the horizon. Your crew is there manning their stations. Everything is shipshape and Bristol fashion. They all gaze at you in expectation. 'Well, Captain,' they seem to say, 'what now?'

If you have done your preparation well, that should all have been taken care of. Everyone should know their duties, be aware of where everything is on the stand and be highly motivated. In practice, however, there will always be things that need attending to and latecomers to brief.

Hopefully, in the first hour a few prospects will arrive to get things off to a good start. Then, if the show is a good one, things move into steady rhythm. Your voyage has started. You can relax a little. Until your next possible crisis – the visit of the Argonaut and his entourage.

So let's look at what makes a stand work smoothly and efficiently.

■ Discipline

While exhibiting should be fun, there has to be a firm hand on the tiller. Not only might members of staff arrive with the attitude that an exhibition is an excuse for a three-day binge, but it will usually be the first time the team has worked together.

I find that, as with any undertaking, when things are going well there is little trouble, but if a show is poorly attended or your company is going through hard times, disputes break out and resentment festers. The main solution is to ensure that everybody is kept occupied, so there is little time for those little groups to form and chat menacingly over coffee. Maybe you need to invent seemingly meaningful tasks, just like POWs digging tunnels at Stalag Luft III.

■ The least likely people often behave badly

Who are the worst offenders? There is no doubt that salespeople know how to let their hair down when they get together. You could even use a 'rumpus' as the collective noun for representatives. But, although they play hard, they also work hard. I have found deskbound staff to be much worse. Once off the leash, they run wild. Of all groups at events, I have heard that bank managers are the most unruly, one group of them having earned the distinction of being the most disruptive group ever to visit the Blackpool Pleasure Beach. It's possibly apocryphal, but I can believe it. Just an aside – how is it that bank managers get the lowest rates of insurance on their cars when they scare the living daylights out of you if they ever give you a lift?

■ Status

Apart from company directors and very senior managers, who naturally demand deference and a certain amount of forelock-tugging, rank ceases to be relevant at the show. It matters little how much a person earns or what company car he or she drives. I have had arguments with sales managers about who should control their field staff when on site. Exhibiting is a great leveller. It must be made clear from the outset that all are equal under you or the stand manager, if that is someone else.

■ Delegate Duties

Stands, like any other business entities, need managers. Apart from the overall responsibilities of the stand manager, the areas that can be delegated are:

- Health and safety.
- Catering (if you choose not to take my advice, and have food and drink).
- Collateral support (print, samples and merchandise).
- Demonstrations and live elements.
- Communications with the office.
- The press room.
- Business records.

I try to give everybody something to do. It promotes a feeling of involvement.

■ Roster and Shift System

There is always a temptation, especially with smaller firms, to keep as many people on the stand as possible at all times. This is especially true if they are earning commission from sales. For every stand, there is a correct staffing level, and exceeding it is counterproductive. There will be too little space for visitors, and a block of clipboard-wielding salespeople will be intimidating. But those off-duty must be given gainful employment if they are not to get into mischief. Yes, it is just like school.

■ The pattern of the day

Every venue and every show has its own characteristic pattern of attendance and traffic flow. Try to work this out in advance. Much of it is common sense, but it's worthwhile chatting to the organisers. Work out how many will be needed on the stand for each segment of the day.

For the first hour, you won't need very many. Then as the crowds arrive, traffic increases and so should your ability to handle it. Some shows have a dip at lunchtime as visitors move towards the grazing grounds. Others don't. The last hour of the day can also be slack, but while you may not need a full team, having a heavyweight on hand is a sound policy as visitors in a buying mood often spend the day looking at the options open to them, then make a decision just before leaving. Or if undecided they will return to review their shortlist.

■ Breaks

If your staff are doing their jobs properly, they will be under intense pressure and will require breaks. Meal breaks are unavoidable, but it is better to have several short ones, rather than one long lunch break. Breaks can be productive in other ways. In addition to meal breaks, encourage them to tour the show and especially look at competitors' stands. This way they will gain a greater perspective on the industry.

■ Matching teams

Teamwork is vital for effective exhibiting. With every new and inexperienced salesperson there should always be someone who can answer a tricky question or make a difficult decision. However, you should check from time to time to make sure that bad habits are not being learnt along with the good ones.

When exhibiting abroad, local staff are an asset

Try also to make up teams of mixed skills and areas of expertise. At an international show abroad, try to ensure that you have somebody on the stand at all times who speaks the host nation's language, even if the industry standard is English. There will always be a local electrician who insists on disconnecting you. A few well-chosen expletives in the local vernacular will soon send him packing.

On the other hand, there are some arrangements to avoid: Don't let life-long buddies band together, especially if they haven't seen each other for a time. They will spend the day chatting and want to take their breaks together. It's also not a good idea to split the staff into all male and all female teams.

■ Handovers

When teams change, there should be a formal handover procedure. It should cover:

- Keys.
  The duty stand manager is responsible for the keys at all times.
- Stand log.
  The stand log should be brought up to date and signed.
- Notice of appointments, important visitors and VIPs expected.
  Naturally you will have a timetable posted on your noticeboard. If there are any last-minute changes warn the incoming team.

■ Responsibilities

Nobody likes responsibilities. And everybody has a good reason to slide out of the job. 'Sorry, I'm allergic to dust...' 'Can't do that, old chap, I won't be here on Friday...' and the favourite of all, 'Not with my bad back.'

Just explain that many hands make light work. If the jobs are divided up fairly, usually nobody has anything too arduous or too time-consuming to do. Except for you, the stand manager, of course. You'll always have more than enough on your plate, however much you delegate.

Here are some of the jobs you can delegate to make your life easier:

- Health and safety officer.
- Standards manager (stand cleanliness and tidiness, staff smartness, retouching scuffed paintwork).
- Collateral manager (literature and giveaways).
- Catering manager.
- Recorder (logging leads, arranging appointments).
- Demonstrations and presentations manager.
- HR manager (rosters, transport, accommodation, late meals etc.).

■ Make a Full Inventory

As soon as your stand is complete, make a full inventory of everything. Apart from making sure that everything is ready for action, there will be no case for recriminations later.

■ The potted plant story

'Who remembers that potted plant by the counter?' It still resonates in my mind, especially as it has happened to me more than once. The man from the hire company stands with a supercilious smirk. He, too, has heard it many times. He has no cause to worry, because his company has a signature for it.

'I'm sure it was here when we arrived,' a voice chirps up more in hope than certainty, from the person you put in charge of flowers and greenery.

Long, long ago, when it first happened, there was no alternative but to stump up for the costliest potted plant in England. Of course, now I just pull out my inventory and can confirm that it wasn't there at the start. It is at this point that you notice a flash of greenery disappearing in the direction of your neighbours' van. When you ask to see the signature on the hire company's docket, it reads 'Joe Bloggs'. The sneaky sods next door had it all the time.

Your inventory should include not just the item name, but details of the supplier and a contact address. If something needs replacing or mending in a hurry, that's the place to look for the telephone number you need.

■ Check consumables and literature before leaving each evening

Of course, you will have assigned somebody to do that, unless it's a very small stand with just a couple of you running it. Even if somebody is made responsible, I would still double-check how much you will need for the next day.

On the first day there is rarely a problem. Most stands are grossly overstocked with everything. But it's worth keeping a record of what has been used, so that you know how much to bring with you from the hotel room or get from your truck.

Literature is a primary concern. A person sent back to collect replenishments is a person not selling. Be prepared for rushes on literature, like after you have done a press launch in the main arena.

Small items are frequently forgotten: pens and pads on the reception desk, batteries for handsets and microphones, and gaffer tape.

■ The press office

Don't forget the press office when replenishing. It's worth checking several times a day if it is unsupervised. Apart from replenishment, the stacks of literature need to be tidied frequently. Dare I mention deliberate sabotage? I've never caught anyone at it, but on some shows, literature seems to disappear at an alarming rate and much seems to end up on the floor or in the waste bin. Would we resort to such underhand tactics? Never.

■ Staff matters

At the show, in addition to everything else, the stand manager is the HR manager. You will have to deal with everything from lost passports, through sourcing dentists to embarrassing personal matters. You have to be patient, understanding and firm.

■ Contracted staff

Agency staff vary greatly in quality. Generally speaking, the larger agencies are more reliable because they have a reputation to maintain and a larger pool of freelance labour. You can find their names in any event directory. However, most agencies hire out people for a variety of functions, so you should stipulate that any staff supplied must have exhibition experience, preferably with the type of show you are attending. The process will be very efficient, a bit reminiscent of hiring furniture and potted plants. They may give you a choice of people, but you really have to rely on their judgement. To be fair, they are normally right.

■ Smaller agencies

There is, however, one aspect that moves me towards the smaller agencies. They have fewer staff, but they may seem friendlier and more amenable. After the first time of hiring from them, you may build up a relationship with the people they supply. In turn they will identify with you and your company when they are with you. With the large agencies, you may not be able to insist on rehiring staff that you have used before.

For this reason I like to go back to two or three small agencies. With one, the boss even takes her turn, so she is totally aware of my needs. I then can have confidence that she will allocate Sonya or Kate for my reception desk and other people I know for other jobs. They've done it before, so it saves in training and I know they are 100 per cent reliable.

■ Part of the team

I book agency staff into the same hotel and they are treated exactly like any other member of the team. Off the stand, we are all on first-name terms so there is no 'us' and 'them'. The worst case of this I remember was by a large multinational client who should have known better. In this case, mime artists were used on the stand. They were billeted in an inferior hotel some way away from the regular staff and had no transport of their own. The regulars refused to drive them back, so they had to take taxis. The next morning they asked for the fares to be refunded, but the stand manager refused, saying the amount was exorbitant and should be met from their fees. Although the matter was resolved, needless to say a gulf developed and remained to the end of the show, despite efforts to patch matters up.

■ Fast start

It doesn't matter which approach you take. Agency people have to 'hit the ground running'. You have to get them working efficiently as soon as possible. We've all seen the contracted hostess who turns up on the first morning in an ill-fitting uniform with a totally dazed look. She has had no prior briefing and probably knows absolutely nothing about the company. So, in addition to bringing them along to your training day, you should keep agency staff in the loop from the earliest point you can. Send them information about the company and the exhibition. Outline their duties and what you expect from them.

■ Briefing contracted staff

If it's unavoidable that you don't meet contracted staff before the event, try to spend half an hour with them on the first morning or delegate a fairly senior person to do so. Personally introduce them to all on the stand. They can make such a difference to your performance. I have been on stands where after a couple of days, agency hostesses were answering quite searching enquiries and taking a lot of pressure off the sales staff.

■ Receptionists and hosts/hostesses

A receptionist's duties are obvious, but they do need to know where things are and who is who. The function of a host or hostess is slightly less obvious. I would suggest they are to:

■ Help visitors to find their way around the stand and offer solutions to simple queries that don't require interviews.

- Introduce visitors with specialist enquiries to the person most likely to meet their needs.
- Introduce serious prospects to the relevant sales staff. If all sales staff are busy, either make appointments for later or keep their attention until a salesperson becomes free.
- Provide the relevant literature for those who ask.
- Log casual visitors who don't warrant a sales conversation.
- Relieve the receptionist during breaks.
- Ensure leaflet racks, etc. are replenished.
- Hand out promotional fliers or giveaways to passers-by.

Hotels and billeting

Having expressed my preference for the smaller, cosier type of hotel, I am only too aware that most companies will book into a Holiday Inn, Hyatt or Ramada where they have an account. The main thing is to get everyone staying at the same place if at all possible. Better one large impersonal hotel than several small comfortable ones, if only for your peace of mind.

The work for you and your team doesn't end when the show shuts its doors in the evening. You need to meet and debrief. You can, of course, do this in the bar, as many seem to do. I prefer not to let my competitors know if we have had a bad day or that we are having difficulty securing a major contract, so I try to arrange for the temporary use of a meeting room. If there are only a few of you, hold the meeting in your bedroom.

What do you do about the member of staff who has relatives living nearby and would like to stay with them? This is a difficult one, because you don't want to cause resentment. My inclination is to say that everyone is there to do a job, and that job extends after show hours. So the team should all stay together. However, you can allow him or her adequate time to visit.

Backwards and forwards

Transportation between hall and hotel doesn't normally cause major problems if everybody gets on well. It can be awkward if there is anyone in the team that the others dislike intensely or if there is great rivalry. Car rotas get ignored and people get left behind.

■ Car rotas

Everyone likes to take their cars to exhibitions. And they like to use them all the time. If they did so, the roads around the site would be permanently gridlocked. Parking at shows is costly. Common sense tells us that we should reduce the traffic to a minimum. This means organising a show transport rota. Logically the largest cars should be the ones used, but it usually ends up with the salespeople's cars that do all the work because the managers have other agendas.

■ Duty car

Every day you should appoint a duty car as a general runabout. This is the only car that will be available for errands and airport runs. To control its use, there should be a booking form. This helps to avoid duplicated and trivial journeys.

■ Minibuses

If you have any have doubts about staff transportation, hire a minibus. There are many other advantages, not the least being that if you all go out for the evening, only one person has to avoid drinking. A minibus has a much greater capacity than a car, so if you need to pick up a group of important prospects from the airport or collect a heavy package of print, it doesn't divert resources from the stand.

■ Expenses and how to manage them

Approaches to expenses vary from company to company. Some ask staff to put their exhibition expenses on their normal expense accounts. It's very convenient for an exhibition manager, who can wash his hands of them completely. However, it is much more sensible from a control point of view to run separate expense accounts for the exhibition. You need to know what exhibiting at a show really costs the company. We all know that normally frugal people act completely out of character during an exhibition. Minibars are raided, taxis are hired for walkable distances and extravagant meals are consumed at Indian restaurants.

■ No-no expenses

Wherever you are and however well you think you know every-body, you have to 'read the riot act' at the start of the show. It is not a free-for-all at the company's expense. You need to list what is and is not allowed. Here are some of the stipulations I have made over the years:

- All alcoholic drinks from the hotel minibar must be paid for.
- One daily newspaper is allowed.
- The only taxi fares allowed are between hotel and station or air-port unless otherwise authorised.
- An allowance of £50 will be allowed for entertaining customers and prospects during the show. This is extendable if a justifiable case is made.
- Evening meals consumed outside the hotel are not allowable.
- Breakfasts taken outside the hotel are allowable, as are sand-wiches and snacks at midday.
- One bottle of wine is allowed with an evening meal at the hotel per person.

■ Per diems

The alternative is to say that only bed and breakfast at the hotel will be paid for. The rest has to be met by a flat rate 'per diem' (Latin for 'daily') allowance paid in cash at the start of the show. This arrangement used to be quite common, but has fallen into disuse of late. It has much to commend it, not least in budgetary control. It also tends to encourage sobriety since the money not spent can be taken home. Of course, you do get the colourful char-acters who manage to spend it all in the first day or so, and have to be 'subbed' for the rest of the show, but then they are trouble what-ever system you run.

■ Time Management

Anyone who has worked on an exhibition stand will tell you that activity ranges from zero, when every person approaching is pounced upon, to intense activity, when you wonder if you will be able to cope. Much of this tidal flow of humanity is predictable and you can plan accordingly, but sometimes it isn't and you are faced with an overwhelming number of visitors clamouring for your attention. Worse still, they may all be quality prospects that you need to process efficiently.

■ What to do in slack periods

For some reason, these always occur when the Argonaut decides to visit.

'Thought you told me this a show that everybody came to,' he casually remarks. 'Not many here now.'

You know your response should be everything but casual. 'Done really well so far, Jason. It's a temporary lull,' you reply hopefully, knowing he isn't convinced. You certainly don't feel inclined to remind him that attending was his suggestion.

Let's see what we can do about those boring slack periods, usually first thing in the morning and during lunchtime. When you walk round a show at these times you notice that on some stands the staff are lounging around, doing crosswords and nursing hangovers. On others, they are tweaking their equipment or finding useful work like tidying literature to occupy their time. Yet others are actually serving what few visitors there are. How come this last group are using their time profitably when the others are not?

It's often quite simple. They have taken measures to attract people to their stand.

■ Appointments

Maybe they have anticipated these slack periods and used them for appointments previously made with customers. This is an ideal time to deal with the host of lesser buyers you need to talk to at some time during the show. Call them up before the show and arrange meetings at the beginning of the day. If you say it is much better then because you can give them more time with fewer interruptions, many will appreciate this personal attention.

■ PR events

You can also use these periods for PR events like contract signings. Press activity heats up during the day, and although you may miss some of the journalists who keep gentlemen's hours, the trade press are normally there for the duration and take a professional view. If there is more time to talk and take photos, you get more coverage.

■ Workshop sessions

You could run special workshop sessions. I know companies who have done this successfully. They have invited technical buyers along to listen to the company boffin expound on future developments or ways to enhance performance. If you have the space and resources, short ten-minute sessions can be very rewarding and give depth of support in customer companies.

■ Promotions

If you anticipate that there will be slack periods but cannot predict when they will be, take measures to stimulate interest. Have minor promotions in reserve that can quickly be put into action. An example could be a draw for 20 copies of a desirable software package that your company produces. Send out hostesses to give out tickets stating that a draw will take place in half an hour's time on your stand. Recipients will swarm to your stand if there is a chance of something free. It matters little that the software is an outdated version that costs you nothing.

It is not difficult to use a little creative thought to come up with a scheme that will attract people. The strange thing is that even after you have drawn the winners, the buzz round your stand will last for some time.

■ Fishing

If there are a few visitors meandering aimlessly around, you might as well get them to visit your stand. Who knows, one or two might turn out to be potential customers. As a matter of fact, this is not so far-fetched as it seems. Many buyers have a very blinkered view of their supplier pool. They tend not to think laterally. It is quite feasible that you might strike lucky with one of these casual passers-by. However, they will not visit you because you are not on their list. How do you get them to come aboard?

It is known as 'fishing'. You move a couple of your staff off the stand and out into the aisle. I call them 'catchers' because that's what they do. This is frowned upon by the organisers because they claim it restricts traffic flow, but if there is little traffic what is the problem? It is surprisingly easy to engage people in conversation when there isn't much activity.

Something else you may well discover is how many potential customers had not intended to visit your stand. It is only when you ask what their needs are that you find there are mutual interests. Most will not be first-level prospects, but some may be. I have several times contacted passers-by who subsequently became major buyers. They were not aware of the full range of our products or thought we were too expensive until that conversation.

So slack periods are not an excuse for everybody to wander off 'for a quick puff'. They can be turned into busy periods with a little forethought.

■ The busy periods

Hopefully you will have more than your fair share of busy periods too. No cause for concern there. You just get stuck in, don't you? Well, yes, but it helps if you've planned your approach beforehand.

Picture the scene. There are four of you on duty and there are perhaps ten visitors wandering about your stand. The hostesses are doing their bit of filtering out the serious from the merely curious. If they are good, they will be directing the prospects into holding areas and keeping them busy until a salesperson becomes available. If you are one of the salespeople, you realise the pressure on you to complete your pitch and move on to the next, so that those waiting don't drift away.

To be able to deal with this type of situation professionally needs preparation and acquired skill. You will never get it completely right, but the following selection of techniques might help.

■ Selling on a Stand

■ A different kind of salesmanship

It is a common misconception that if you can sell in the field, you can sell on an exhibition stand. Several excellent salespeople have arrived on stands that I have run thinking that they will have an easy time, only to discover that the techniques honed over years of visiting buyers in their offices don't work.

When you are on a stand you have to have a very disciplined approach. In the few minutes at your disposal:

- A relationship has to be made,
- the customer's needs established,
- a response to those needs outlined,
- further action committed to,
- the customer's details logged.

■ Six minutes

I suggest you aim to complete a pitch in six minutes. To achieve that, time management is clearly crucial. You have to use the six minutes effectively and close with a positive outcome and a logged result. Then disengage swiftly. If you don't, becoming engrossed in detail and missing your deadline, means you will miss the person waiting in the wings who might turn out to be a major new buyer.

If you did role-playing on your mock stand during your training, you'll remember how your staff begged to be given more time for each pitch. On the first few attempts, they would just be getting into their stride when you told them to draw to a close. They found the exercise frustrating.

■ Committing your time

Of course, the six minutes is an average. Sometimes it will be four and sometimes eight. It obviously depends on how crowded the stand is and how the pitch is progressing. The first thing you have to do when confronted by a smiling, eager person is decide how much time your prospect is worth. We have already established that your sales pitch has to be distilled from what would normally take at least half an hour into about a fifth of the time. It helps to practise beforehand.

You need to assess:

- If you are the right person for the prospect to be talking to. If they are interested in technical or distribution matters outside your experience, pass them to the specialist or make an appointment without delay.
- Their awareness of your company and range. A totally new prospect will need to know more than an established customer.
- Their buying power. The size of the company and the prospect's function and status within it.
- How much do they need to know at this time? Even if the prospect is a major buyer, this may not be the right time for a big sales push. A decision may not be needed for six months.

You have only 20 seconds to decide. Practise through observation. It is important that you make this commitment to your prospect.

■ Introduce yourself and take the lead

Always open by introducing yourself and finding out the prospect's identity and who they work for. It is amazing how many salespeople forget this, and indeed I frequently do so in the heat of the moment. It is so easy to get sidetracked by a prospect who is determined to lead the conversation.

'So you're International Spigots', he starts, glancing round the stand. 'Where are you based?' Try not to get carried away by his enthusiasm. Avoid merely responding to his questions – you'll end up knowing very little about him until at the end he hands you his card. Worst of all, there will be no opportunity to close. You and your salespeople must learn the art of politely taking the lead and guiding the conversation in the right direction.

■ The sales story

We've all met the car salesman who assails you with talk of over-head camshafts and intercoolers. Undoubtedly there are enthusiasts who make buying decisions on the basis of how many valves or injectors there are, but I don't know any. I suspect that even boy racers are more impressed by external shiny bits than what is under the bonnet. People buy cars for a variety of motives, performance being only one.

However illogical it may seem, a final car-buying decision some-times come down to the colour of the upholstery or the quality of the sound system. What the car salesperson should be selling is not the car as a piece of metal, but the pleasure of ownership of the car. If you like, the difference that car will make to the new owner's life.

The same is true for selling on exhibition stands. Listening to sales-people on stands, I often feel that they forget everything they have learnt in the field. There on the stand is a big shiny machine, so they launch into eloquent monologues about what is 'under the bonnet', something they wouldn't do when visiting a customer.

Maybe they feel that in distilling the story into several minutes, there is no time for the seductive touch.

■ The ALERT principle

Isn't it funny how we in sales like to reduce everything to clever acronyms. Here's another specially designed for exhibition stands. It also helps in time management:

1 **Ask.**

Open by asking questions about the prospect's needs and aspirations.

2 **Listen.**

Listen to the replies, without commenting (unless the prospect is wasting valuable time, when a gentle verbal nudge may be necessary to get back on track).

3 **Empathise.**

Identify with those needs, any problems and future difficulties. Show the prospect that you are on their side and have the experience to help.

4 **Respond.**

Reply with your company's solution, in terms of product, service and terms of business.

5 **Take action and record details.**

Turn the prospect into a productive contact, by booking an appointment, factory visit, demonstration or entry on a tender list. Then make sure that you have recorded every pertinent detail of your conversation.

If you reckon on a minute for each of those topics, you end up with a five-minute sales pitch. If you add in another minute to cover an extra important question, that makes six minutes, just about right for a casual visitor.

■ Parrots need not apply

There was one aspect of selling on a stand that I used to hate when I first started. That was being instructed to learn the story off a script and tell it to all visitors parrot-fashion. My colleagues and I soon grew sick of repeating the same claptrap time after time, just like those people at call centres must. We embellished it and added jokes, as much as anything to keep our sanity. I now know that pre-prepared pitches are a complete waste of time. You soon cease to be persuasive, just like the call centres.

Anyway, there are better ways of communicating the standard company line in information. Videos, display boards and touch screens aren't expected to have personalities and more suited to the task.

■ Really interested people (RIPs)

If the prospect is showing serious interest and is 'flashing buying signals', then you have to move into different mode. Then you can spend more time in the inner sanctum of the 'chat area', if you have one.

Inform your staff so that they can cover for you, then retire to set about your serious business conversation. Once again, set yourself a time limit and mentally work towards that objective of a positive result.

The acronym RIP is handy to write in the log and stands out well when reviewing business.

■ The itch

I said some way back that done deals are not often effected on exhibition stands, unless you are in the T-shirt, mobile phone or kitchen knife businesses. But you are there to make that first positive step in the process that will result in an order. Many salespeople do very well initially, putting the sales story succinctly and persuasively, but they fail to do the equivalent of a close. They must initiate the sales process with a commitment from the prospect. So how do you do that?

I call it the 'itch'. An itch is something that pesters you. The itch you are trying to plant is a desire for ownership. And it is this desire for ownership that must itch like mad whenever the prospect is frustrated by a problem at work that your product can solve. It must also itch when competitors sing the praises of their naturally inferior products. It must itch when budgets are being formulated.

A good itch sells for you even when you are not present.

■ The sand in the oyster's shell

What is the grain of sand that initiates the itch under the prospect's shell? Only you will be able to work that out. Suffice to say that it has to fit into that tiny parcel of time after you have listened to the prospect's needs and empathised with them. It has to be something that the prospect will take away in his or her brain, to irritate and develop into a valuable pearl of business.

Exhibitions are unique in that they offer opportunities for all the senses. They allow countless exciting ways to stimulate desire that cannot be achieved in other media. Prospects can handle products, they can be guided through simple case studies on video, they can feel the vibration of a working machine at a demonstration, and they can even smell the oil. Touch is an especially strong stimulant to a desire for ownership. Just watch shoppers in Next. Feeling the garments is as important as looking at them. When you handle something, you can imagine it in your possession. Emotive stimuli all help to guide the prospect into ownership mode and generate desire.

If you can, get your sales staff to expand their selling techniques to include all these almost subconscious nuances. There will probably never be as good an opportunity ever again to get that itch itching.

■ The soothing balm

For every itch there is a soothing balm. Your product range is it. Our task as salespeople is to be accessible when the balm is needed. This is where the concept of 'productive contacts' comes in handy.

Despite the fact that on most trade show stands a salesperson will not have the opportunity to 'close' in the conventional sense, my staff are expected to end every pitch with a serious prospect by a positive action. That positive action must include a commitment. Positive actions could be:

- An appointment to meet a senior executive or technical director later at the show.
- A sales appointment at the prospect's premises.
- An opportunity to make a capability presentation or business proposal.
- A visit to your factory.
- A confirmed opportunity to tender for the next contract.

The important thing is that when you leave the show, an ongoing relationship has been established.

■ Using the chat area

Everybody calls them 'chat areas'. That is really the last thing they should be called. It implies something akin to a fundraising coffee morning. I suppose 'keenly focused personal presentation suites' sounds pretentious, but it would be a better description.

When you take a prospect or customer to whatever it is you decide to call it, you are doing so for a purpose. Maybe it will be an extension to your six minutes. You discovered that there was more than a passing interest that justified probing deeper. Possibly an old customer dropped by wanting to sort out a quality problem or discuss next year's discounts.

Inevitably such meetings take longer than six minutes, but they should not degenerate into long discussions best left for after the show. Tell your visitor that you can allocate just 15 minutes to the meeting, which must either end in resolution or be continued on another occasion. Keep it all tight and meet your deadline.

■ Chat area discipline

There has to be discipline in the use of chat areas. If they are to justify the space they occupy, they should be in constant use. So anyone overstaying their time is penalising somebody else.

You should also have a booking system for appointments, which must have priority. Before settling in for an intense discussion with a new acquaintance, glance at the appointments book. If a booking is imminent, do the booker the courtesy of taking your visitor to the coffee bar rather than causing them embarrassment. Or why not make an appointment with them so you can talk when there is less pressure?

Chat areas should be equipped for business meetings with all the resources you are likely to need. Few forget to install a coffee machine, but often there is no bookshelf containing current price lists and folders of technical specifications.

■ Called to the bar

Strangely there is rarely any problem in getting sales staff to take customers to the bar. I wonder why? Exhibition bars are quite good places to do business, provided there is sufficient room. You and your customer can discuss business informally and with fewer distractions than on the stand, helping to cement your relationship.

'How about a discussing it over a swift bevvy?' When you hear that, take note of who is offering. With some people it won't be quite so swift and there will be more bevvying than business. Visits to the bar should be restricted. If not, they become more and more inebriated as the day progresses.

■ Chasing invitees, customers and friends

When we looked at marketing, I suggested measures for inviting customers and contacts to your stand. Surprisingly, even having been invited, few actually make the effort unless chased or given some incentive.

If you have their mobile phone numbers, call them or send them texts to remind them. If possible, give them a reason to come.

■ Getting rid of 'campers'

Everybody gets them from time to time. Visitors who interpret your cheery welcome as an invitation to stay and chat for ages. If they can get a free coffee out of you, so much the better. Many are sad souls who seek company. It is difficult not to be sympathetic. Nevertheless, they take up valuable space and have to be removed.

This is a job for the hosts or hostesses. They should be briefed to gently remove such people. The technique is easy to master and can be quite painless. Normally it is just a matter of asking what they want to see next and guiding them on their way.

■ Gauging Success

'Look out, everybody, he's on his way.'

The moment you've been dreading. The Argonaut's visit. Your strategically placed spy has returned to inform you that you have at most a minute or two to get everything up to scratch. Then the great man and his entourage arrive like some minor royal. He sniffs the air, casts a critical eye over your displays and raps his fingers on the counter top.

'Splendid. Couldn't have done better myself.' The PR person at his side reminds him of a photo opportunity in a couple of minutes and he is away again.

Success! You can sleep easy. Your P45 has been put on hold for another year.

■ The real success

But is the stand really performing in the business sense? It is not always easy to tell. In the average show, waves of visitors wash over you. Sometimes you are busy, sometimes slack. Even if your stand is constantly busy and you seem to be working your socks off, you may find in the final reckoning that you have not achieved enough productive contacts.

On very busy stands, insufficient time and attention is given to prospects. Even the business cards collected are not necessarily a good measure of success. Lots will be from the trade press, competitors and PR agencies after your business. Many of the people you met may not be the decision-makers.

On the other hand, quiet stands can yield extremely good results. This is because if the quality of the visitors is high, you don't need many of them and can devote more time to them.

Gut feeling is often a poor gauge of stand performance. So how do you assess how you are doing?

■ Debriefing

The answer is to monitor business on a daily basis. In the evening, hold a debriefing session. Go through the log and see who in the team is the most productive and who needs to improve. If you are not hitting targets, find out why.

Maybe you feel your team isn't trying hard enough. If this is so, it's no use demoralising them by using threats. Better to issue incentives and give them something desirable to aim for. Appeal to their competitive spirit by dividing them into teams.

Possibly it isn't their fault. It happens. A railway strike or terrorist attacks can decimate attendance. Maybe it was not an event you should have booked in the first place. You just have to make the best of a bad job. Enlist the help of the troops. Brainstorm. Often they will come up with the most original ideas.

■ Seek reasons from the log

Frequently the same comments from visitors recur many times in the log: 'economic downturn', 'new technological breakthrough expected any day now' and 'cheap foreign competition' are common ones. In such circumstances, it is worth discussing an answer among yourselves on the principle that any objection is a sales opportunity.

For every negative viewpoint there is a positive answer. In many cases these comments are pure excuses to terminate the conversation. In others they may signify deeply-felt frustration with the state of the industry or market place, and warrant investigation. If you are allowed to look into the prospect's problems, it's possible you might be able to find a solution.

■ Cutting costs and adding value

Often you can propose a solution through cutting costs or adding value. If you can offer those, you are in with a chance. Let's look at possible answers to those objections:

- Economic downturn.

  Answer – all business is cyclical. While you might not want to be spending heavily at the moment, this is the time to prepare for the upturn. You know, Mr Customer, that the first off the mark when the upturn comes will be the winner. Let us come and help you prepare for a fast getaway when you decide to reinvest.

- Imminent technical change.

  Answer (depending heavily on whether you are a technological leader or not) –

  1. Technological change needs to be prepared for. You, Miss Customer, should talk to our engineers now to plan for a smooth and seamless transfer when the time comes. As a matter of fact, we have machines using transitional technology that will keep your market happy during the switch.

  2. It will take some years for the new technology to be fully adopted. Our advice is to let the others have the mental breakdowns and spend millions making it work. Then jump in with proven solutions. In the interim, our solution is solid and cost-effective. You'll be able to maintain a solid customer base while they are disappointing theirs.

- Cheap foreign competition.

  Answer – if you can't beat them, join them. If you want to set up a plant in the Philippines or China, we can support you all the way. We're prepared to set up an office in the Far East and we will be able to supply you with plant as soon as you are ready to receive it.

There is an answer to every objection. It's just that our brains do not normally work fast enough to think of it at the time. No matter. If you have a contact address for the person, send a short proposal and an offer to discuss it at their office.

▓ Registering and logging prospects

This is what it's all about. Registering and logging has to be done and done efficiently. If you are exhibiting in a business-to-business environment, you and your staff should get the name and contact number of everyone who sets foot on the stand, whether or not they seem to have any value to your company at the time.

As you sift through the information after the show you will find that all sorts of people whom you should have met have escaped through the holes on your net. The names of well-known freelance journalists and technical gurus probably didn't mean much to the receptionist on the counter so they weren't introduced to anyone important. They are definitely worth a follow-up letter.

Encourage everyone to log as much information as they can on each contact. Even if there isn't time after the interview, get them to add other thoughts afterwards. It's also useful to put in identifying details, like 'tall man in brown corduroy jacket', to jog the memory afterwards.

When I say 'log', it is in reality many logs. All stand staff should have a clipboard on which the details are jotted for later transfer to the main log. I have been on stands that have been so busy that there has not been time to transfer details until the evening debrief. All the more reason to get details down right the first time.

Make certain every logged entry has the name of the salesperson responsible beside it. There are two reasons for this:

- You may need to ask further questions about the lead.
- It is great to be able to compliment the salesperson responsible if the lead turns into real business.

Especially important is to log every person to whom you give literature. Their action in taking your literature is excuse enough for you to call after the show. I like to ring them and ask how useful they are finding the brochure and if there is anything in it that needs explaining. It is amazing how good the response is.

■ Grading contacts

As previously mentioned, I like to grade contacts. It isn't just for future reference, but it becomes a good discipline to judge people immediately after you have spoken to them. The human memory, being what it is, remembers the colourful characters to the detriment of the drab ones. By grading them in an objective way you redress the balance.

The following is a suggested simple grading system:

A – Potential or existing customer with orders imminent and serious interest.

B – Potential or existing customer keen to establish relationship for future business.

C – Possible new customer expressing genuine interest.

D – Curious prospect worth following up.

E – Visitor worth noting for the future.

F – No-hoper.

You can also add grades for size of business and country of origin. Avoid making the grading too complex or it defeats the object. A little tip – also keep a note of the no-hopers. It could save you time chasing them in the future.

▪ Business cards

The international currency of the business world. Most salespeople are only too aware of the need to ask for business cards. Suggest they ask for two if they can get away with it, one for your records and one for the salesperson to keep. If a true relationship has been established with the prospect and the salesperson has handed over their own card, the prospect might easily get in touch at a future date.

Make it a policy to collect cards from everyone, not just those visitors your company is immediately interested in. If you have a good card filing system back at the office, you may be able to trace that funny little man in the brown trilby that you met in Hamburg who knew some 'useful contacts' in Turkey.

▪ Looking at your competitors

The exhibition is a great opportunity to study your competitors. In addition to a close look at their latest ranges, you can collect the latest brochures and price lists.

■ PR and Generating News

'Hi, Tark. Popped down for the launch?' You welcome the agency party arriving led by the irrepressible Tarquin.

'Yes,' he replies. 'Want to see you guys are on the ball. Pity about the bubble gum machine. It would have looked good there.'

They've just been on a tour of the trade press stands spreading the word about the new range. Hopefully they will have been sufficiently persuasive to get you metres of editorial. Somehow you are a little sceptical.

News at exhibitions can be divided into:

- News intended for those who could not attend, to keep them up to date with what they missed.
- News generated at the show to increase visitor awareness of your presence and willingness to visit your stand.

■ News for exterior audiences

Exhibitions are a heaven-sent opportunity to get your stories out. The trade press is constantly on hand and keen to listen to anything newsworthy. On the other hand, there will be a few hundred other companies clamouring for their attention. There are two principles of good press work:

- Make the press's job easy for them.
- Give them something to get their teeth into.

■ Making it easy for the press

The popular conception of an exhibition from a reporter's viewpoint as being one long string of boozy parties interrupted by a few photo calls and embarrassing publicity stunts, is a little short of the truth. The press do try to cover every exhibitor at the show, but there never is enough time.

Exhibitors who achieve good coverage are the ones who have everything neatly packaged. Put yourself in their shoes. If you were sifting through piles of releases with a looming deadline, you'd go for the best-presented press packs.

A good press pack should contain:

- Good photographs, properly captioned.
- Press releases professionally written.
- Support packs with relevant literature.
- Contact names and timetable of best times for interviews.
- Personal invitation to visit the stand.

Many journalists now find it convenient to have editorial and pictures also supplied on CD-ROM, so that they can just cut and paste on their PCs.

Timing

Ideally you want a running programme of stories that maintains interest throughout the show. In practice, you rarely have enough strong ones at a time when everyone else is clamouring for attention and submitting weak stones to fill the gaps does you no favours. Also many publications, in the interests of fairness and no doubt to appease their advertising managers, operate a quota system.

So I like to major on two or three stories, varying the tone and approach. One might be a big product launch, another an impressive contract signing and the third a general interest piece like a technological prediction by the technical director.

One story that succeeded beyond expectations resulted from a visit by a distinguished 95-year-old company director to a stand. He had some wonderful anecdotes about conditions when he was an apprentice. The press loved them.

Incidentally, interesting articles on technical and market matters are often welcomed by the less prestigious magazines that rely on outside contributions to fill their pages. Not only do you get the kudos of becoming a source of expert information, but they will often run off reprints for you.

■ Photography

Submit photographs to support every story filed. There is rarely a topic for which supporting pictures cannot be found.

With the increasing use of colour in printing, it is easy to produce colour prints or files. If the publication wants them in black and white, they can convert them electronically.

Nowadays everything is more flexible and you do not have to be so careful about the format of the pictures. However, here are some tips:

- Captioning.
  Ensure that there is a full description of what is happening and its significance. If people are featured, give their names and titles. The caption should ideally be typed on a sticky label and fixed to the back of the print. Captions written in ballpoint directly onto the back of the print sometimes bleed through and often the indentations show.
- Permission of featured people.
  It is best to try and get the permission from featured people to use their image in the press. This is common courtesy. It is not necessary to gain the permission of the general public if they are going about their normal business in a public place.
- Cropping.
  Keep the picture tight. If you don't crop out all the irrelevant background, the publication will. It is better for you to do it, especially if there is something outside the focal point that is important. Nevertheless, try to keep the proportions reasonable, or they will crop more just to make the picture fit.
- Composition.
  Consider the readers. They want interesting shots, not boring ones contrived by your PR department to satisfy executive egos. If you are featuring people, have them doing something interesting. Merely shaking hands or holding up a certificate is not really enough to get more than a passing glance from readers in a trade paper. Machines should have operators to indicate scale. And choose a working environment over a showroom for pictures of products.

- File types.

  Normally the publication will have a picture specification for pictures submitted electronically. If not, a reasonably high resolution JPEG is the most acceptable for news items.

The pressroom

The pressroom is primarily designed for reporters to collect background information on the companies exhibiting and their products. In the best-run exhibitions, only the press is allowed access. In practice, everybody who submits packs and releases will be in and out keeping their section up to date. Naturally, in passing their competitors' literature, company PROs will collect as much information as they can. The inevitable result is that anything you put in the pressroom is read first by the people you least want to know about it.

This is not to say that you should ignore pressrooms, but anything sensitive should be communicated to the press by more secure means.

It is worth visiting the pressroom at least a couple of times a day to make sure that your stock is tidy and replenished. Many exhibitors are enthusiastic on the first day, then let things drift. Their spaces are taken over by more aggressive neighbours, and of course, any information remaining will be about the least popular items, which does their product range less than credit. Not a good idea image-wise.

Staged events

A few words of warning. What seems exciting to you may not be viewed that way by the press. Events on your stand may be newsworthy, but don't presume that the press will be interested in your celebs or entertainers. A politician will attract reporters in the hope that he will give an insight into party policy during his brief address. If this is reported, the chances are you will only get a minor mention. A contestant from *Big Brother* or *Pop Idol* will rightly be viewed as a publicity stunt and shunned unless copy is very short.

▨ Signings

Contract signings sound dull, but they needn't be. I try to engineer them a bit. A crowd begets a crowd. So I always try to get a group of people (normally stand staff and friends) standing around expectantly, glancing at watches and muttering. More will join them. Then there is a short presentation to give the sales story behind the contract. In the background, a couple of waiters pour champagne into a multitude of glasses, giving the impression that everybody in the vicinity will get one, which they do if they stay to the end. The signing is performed with as much pizzazz as you can muster. Contrived or what? Of course, but it usually works.

▨ Launches

'Roll up, roll up! Come and see the new Model 362! Be amazed at its speed. Marvel at its productivity.' Who said the age of snake oil is past. It is an established adage among copywriters that the two most powerful words in the English language are 'new' and 'free'.

Exhibitions are good places to launch new products. Visitors are eager to be amazed. There is nothing like a well-managed product launch to enhance its reputation as innovative, design-conscious and technically advanced.

A few hints on how to make your product launch a success at the show:

- Remember always that it is the new product that is the star attraction.
- Build expectation by keeping everything as secret as you can, except of course that something dramatic is imminent. Anything that has to be given to the press before the event should have a strict embargo on it. If you want to generate hype, start rumours without giving anything away.
- Give the launch everything you've got. Other companies will also be launching new products, so you are in competition not just in your product grouping but for a share of the show's limelight.

- You are unlikely to have enough space to do everything on the stand, so book rooms for receptions and press conferences.
- Brand everything heavily.
- Keep the new product in context. Unless you are a single product company, on the day after the launch the new product will have to take its place as part of an existing range.
- Don't forget those who can't make the show. Support the launch in other media.

Launches should be great fun, and a good excuse for being over the top. Many events are completely cheesy, but, there is nothing that hasn't been attempted before, so don't rule out unveilings, reveals and tape-cutting. Trumpeters from the Guards still stir the soul. Dry ice still adds an air of mystery. In the world of launches, clichés still rule OK.

■ VIP visits

Something I hate on principle. To me prospects and customers are the VIPs, not some visiting secretary of state, foreign delegation or show business celeb. Unless they happen to also be prospects or customers, of course. Most are doing the grand tour of the show, so have very little interest in you, your stand or your product.

If you have invited a politician to your stand and he or she is prepared to say a few words, you will get press attention if clues are given on a party policy. But your company is hardly likely to be mentioned, unless you engineer it otherwise.

You do, however, have to put on a good show for any VIP visit in the hope that you will get a fleeting mention on the regional TV news. You know the Argonaut will be watching in his hotel suite later in the day. There is only one thing better than his company getting an appearance on the box, and that is him being shown shaking hands with some junior minister.

Visits are something we have to live with. So you had better do the job efficiently. Read the following, and don't say I didn't warn you:

- Make sure your staff are thoroughly briefed on who they are likely to meet. I remember my staff expecting to meet a member of a current chart-topping boy band and being unpleasantly surprised by being introduced to a TV presenter with a similar name.
- Be prepared for VIPs to be late. They invariably are. And usually give no apologies.
- Don't expect the VIPs to know anything about you or your business.
- Expect basic and sometimes idiotic questions from them and their entourage.
- Have a demonstration lined up. Having something to show is easier than trying to hold conversations with people who really don't want to be there.

I am not an overt royalist, but I have to admit that by and large the royal family are the exception to the general pattern of VIPs. They do the job graciously and with dignity, expressing seemingly genuine interest in both people and surroundings.

■ Show newsletters and bulletins

These are probably applicable to large stands with plenty going on, although opinion is divided over their effectiveness. Many are of the view that they take a lot of time and resources to produce, but rarely reach their target audience. Even if they do, nobody has time to read them.

Fair comments. However, they need not be all that difficult to produce with modern desktop publishing and an arrangement with a local digital printing company. One solution is to plan all the editions in advance. Most of what you will do on the stand will be known before you get there, so much of the newsletter can be pre-prepared, leaving gaps for breaking news.

The first two editions will be taken with you already printed. Then you set up your PC in your hotel room on the first evening, download digital images of the stand looking busy, write the stories for the day and email it all to the printer. The next day, they print out your newsletter and deliver it. It is then ready for distribution on the third day.

Distribution can be tackled creatively. If a hotel is accommodating a large number of visitors to the show, ask if they will deliver your newsletter with the newspapers in the morning or have them laid out in reception. At the show, get your hostesses to hand them out to visitors as they arrive. There are many ways to make sure newsletters end up in the right hands if you think about it.

If bulletins are interesting and relevant, they will get read, because they are dynamic when so much of the print material available is static. People love news, especially if they can become involved. If they read that something exciting is going to happen in an hour's time, and they can be there, they will attend.

■ Food and Drink

This is a contentious issue. If you want my view, avoid both like the plague. Any distraction to doing business is to be avoided, and negotiating seriously while trying to balance plastic glasses and munching snacks is not easy. However, you will often be overridden from above and have to provide a bar or snacks. Of course, if your business is food and drink, you have no option.

■ The hospitality café

A phenomenon that seems especially prevalent at county shows is the hospitality café. Perhaps because real estate on the showground is relatively cheap, huge marquees spring up with tables and chairs just so that customers can drop in and have a cup of tea and Belgian bun. Occasionally a rep will pass by and enquire if everything is all right. And that is it. I suppose it is a throwback to more leisurely eras, but it is hardly a productive use of space.

■ Hospitality is for visitors

If you decide to go ahead with food and drink, impress upon your staff that the stand is not a cafeteria for them and their mates. Food and drink are for those prospects and customers who have earned them through expressing interest. When they are actively entertaining, a salesperson may also partake sparingly of what is provided. Nobody can answer a question with dignity with a mouthful of sausage roll.

■ Samples

For those in the food and drink industry, it is obviously very different. Samples are the name of the game. Everyone wants to taste what you have to offer. There is a constant battle keeping up with demand, especially if you have to cook in batches.

The great advantage of marketing food and drink on a stand is that your visitors can actually experience your product, so you can dispense with descriptions and proceed to topics like distribution and price structures.

You will probably be far more acquainted with the technicalities of running kitchens and hotplates on stands than I am. Needless to say, there is a mass of health and safety regulations that pertain just to the preparation of food. You had better take note of it, because there is nothing more embarrassing than being closed down on health and safety grounds. Normally it is an easily correctable technicality that is to blame. I really can't believe that you have to warn visitors that plastic cups containing tea or coffee might be hot to the touch, but it is so.

■ Cultural issues

There are few constraints on the types of food and drink that are acceptable in Europe and the USA, but this is not the case in some parts of the world. Even in countries that claim to be multicultural, there may be high proportions of members of faiths that have strong views on certain foods and alcohol. It such places it is wise to steer clear of controversy.

■ Personnel – own staff or contractors

As with everything in business, there are people waiting to take tedious tasks off your hands at the merest wave of a chequebook. I believe that, if you can afford it, bring in the professionals. Caterers will undoubtedly make a better job of preparing food and serving it. Even if you are serving only wine and cheese – yes, exhibitors do still have retro wine and cheese parties – a professional wine waiter will perform the task with far more aplomb than the average sales-person. Jason the Argonaut is the exception. He not only loves pouring wine and giving all the benefit of his fund of knowledge on wines, but is exceptionally good at it. Company politics aside, the most compelling reason for bringing in caterers is that your staff have better things to do than lay out canapés.

The exception is when you are entertaining just a few people whom you know well and you prefer the atmosphere to be intimate. In such circumstances, when you pour a glass of wine for your cus-tomer you are symbolically doing them a service.

■ Disposables

Jason detests plastic cups, plates and cutlery and has said so on many occasions. As a matter of fact, so do I. They remind me of kids' parties and picnics in the rain.

But on an exhibition stand they are the only real option, unless you have caterers in to clear away afterwards. So plastic it has to be, come what may. I remember a client who was a CAMRA (Campaign for Real Ale) supporter who held a reception on his stand and insisted that proper beer should be served in proper dimple tankards. When it came to returning the glasses, many were missing. Naturally the guests were blamed. However, the glasses turned up over the next day or so, lodged into every conceivable crevice on the stand.

You don't have to settle for the type of polystyrene cups that come from the office water dispenser. There is an array of attractive designs that look just like their glass equivalents.

■ Staff policy on food and drink

Very important. Your staff should be in no doubt about consumption of food and drink on the stand. My rules are:

- No food or drink should be brought in for consumption on the stand. This means no sandwiches or cans of Coke.
- Food and drink provided on the stand are primarily for the use of visitors, and should be consumed only in the company of visitors, except during the last hour of the day when there might be a surplus that would otherwise be thrown away.
- If there is a bar on the stand, all alcoholic drinks should be charged to accounts run for each member of staff. At the end of the show, depending on consumption, the accounts can be waived or invoiced to the drinker's account. When staff realise that there is a chance they may be called upon to pay, they are more careful.

■ Sweets and bon-bons

Great promotional items, especially when cleverly branded. They are small, easily handled, relatively robust and generally acceptable to all visitors. If they are wrapped, provide a receptacle for the papers, or you will find them stuffed into every corner by people who don't wish to be seen leaving litter on your stand.

One idea I especially like is the note that says something like, 'Please take a sweet with our compliments, and leave a business card.' That way you get a tangible return.

■ Smoking

This is a hugely emotive issue. In many western countries, smoking is not allowed in public places, and you can't get much more public than an exhibition hall. Even where this is not the case, the organisers will probably prohibit smoking in the hall.

There are, however, places in the world where the exchange of cigarettes is still a precursor to a business transaction. What do you do there? The best advice is to get informed local opinion. My inclination, and that of other stand managers I know, is to ban smoking on the stand by staff as a matter of principle, but allow visitors to smoke if they have to. Remember to keep ashtrays on hand.

Chapter 17

Getting Out

The last alcoholics have finally been cleared out of the bar. They doors have shut for the last time. The show is over. But it's no time to relax. Everything you did to get your stand here has to be put into reverse gear. You have less time to do it and less help. You've also probably spent all your contingency, so there is nothing in the kitty to 'grease palms' to get you out of any problems.

Impress on all your staff that the show's not over until everything is back in the warehouse. You will find that while there were plenty of people willing to help you build and prepare your stand, there are very few who will help you remove it. It's down to you and the trusty stalwarts from the contractor.

■ The final gathering

It is natural, I suppose, that the moment the show closes its doors, everybody wants to rush off home. They've done their bit. Now they want to get on with all those pressing tasks that have been building up in their absence. What's more, the adrenaline has stopped flowing and they are left with a feeling of anticlimax.

Nevertheless, you need to gather all your staff together for one last time as there are important tasks to be completed before anybody can be allowed to dash for home. Here are some:

- Ensure that everyone's duties are complete and that everything that needs to be signed for is actually signed for.
- Collect all keys, pass cards, company mobile phones and anything else handed out for the duration of the show.

- Ensure that you all have checked out of the hotel and handed in room keys.
- Check that all leads have been recorded in the log and that you have all the business cards that have been collected.
- Find out where your staff will be over the next week or two, in case you want to get in touch with them.
- Check the inventory while the staff are present. Somebody might remember who borrowed a chair or that a monitor was returned to the hire company as being damaged.

The 'get out'

In general, venues allow far too little time for exhibitors to remove stands. The result is blocked accesses, speeding fork-lifts and general mayhem. It is inevitable that things get lost or damaged. However, if you work logically and avoid panicking, you should come out of it relatively unscathed.

Your first action should be to clear the stand of everything you brought with you, either by taking it back with you or consigning it to the skip. It is quite normal to find that you don't have the space in your car or van to carry everything that has accumulated, so you have to ditch things you would like to keep. Do, however, check that nothing confidential finds its way into rubbish bins. Especially if you are abroad, watch out for credit card payment slips and envelopes with addresses.

Protect fragile items immediately

Pack away the fragile equipment in its flight cases immediately the show closes. In addition to protecting it from damage, bulky flight cases present more of a problem to the light of touch. They are also easy to identify if they find their way onto somebody else's truck.

Normally you will want to keep your display boards for further shows. They are a big investment. Unfortunately they are also probably quite fragile, with just foamboard backing. Other people may not realise their value and will knock into them or put heavy objects on them. So make sure that they are properly wrapped up and put out of harm's way.

■ Hired items

Put all the hired items that will be picked up at the venue in the centre of the stand. I recommend putting labels on them, so that there is no confusion if the hire people come round while you are attending to something else. Also keep your file containing the delivery docket to hand. Then there can be no dispute.

■ When the contractors set to

'Steady, you guys. Nothing moves till I give the word.' You catch Gordon walking off with part of the counter.

Naturally the contractors want to get on the road as quickly as possible. But don't let them start dismantling until you are ready. Once the structure starts to come down, you have very little chance of finding anything that is lost. They certainly set to with a will.

The contractors will probably have worked out a loading sequence for their truck. They openly welcome your token offer of help, but realistically you are probably more trouble than you are worth. So stick to carrying manageable components to and fro rather than encroaching on their territory. Leave the heavy bits to them.

While I have found contractors great workers, setting to with a will means that they often take less care than you would like with bits of the stand you will need again. Their attitude is that the whole thing needs to be refurbished back at the works anyway, so what the hell? My attitude is that refurbishment time is chargeable, so the less of it I have to pay for the better. Normally there is a compromise. They are more careful while I am watching and presumably carry on as normal when I am not, since the refurbishment bill never seems to go down.

■ Check for unpaid bills

Before leaving, check the venue, organisers and hotels for unpaid bills and unfinished business. These things are easier to settle on site than two months later when nobody can remember the details.

■ Psychological issues after the show

An interesting topic. Naturally there is an immediate feeling of relief that you survived unscathed . . . if you did. There is a short period of euphoria. You did well and your colleagues tell you so.

Then, as the adrenaline flow reverts to normal, you experience anticlimax. You might even experience the exhibitor's version of post-natal depression. Did it really go as well as all that? You think of the missed opportunities. You question the wisdom of some of your decisions and become self-critical. This you will have to come to terms with. The important thing is not to do anything drastic during this period.

A short time after the dust has settled and you can look back objectively, write down a list of what went well and what will have to be improved next time.

Chapter 18

Post-show Activity

The email flashes up on your screen. 'Great show evrybody. Lets meet up in The Crown and celebrate. Jason.' The Argonaut can neither spell nor use Spell Check. Still the sentiment is there.

You all pile into the bar in the anticipation of a free round from the boss. Big mistake. He never shows up, as usual. All you get is a text to say that he is 'otherwse dtaind'. Nobody really minds as everyone enjoyed the show and there is a fund of amusing show stories to enjoy. The party neatly brings the whole show chapter to a close.

A couple of weeks afterwards, your sighs of relief are merely a memory and everything is back to normal around the office. There is the occasional remark at the water cooler about the great night out or a burgeoning romance between an agency girl on the stand and the Midlands area manager. Otherwise the show is just part of corporate history.

That's how it appears on the surface. This is the time, though, to start to harvest the fruits of your labour. Your small empire has become something akin to MI6, a high-powered intelligence cell analysing and disseminating information to far-flung parts of the company. This is when the real value of your feverish activity on the stand can be assessed.

▧ The debriefs

The first events to be arranged following an exhibition are the two debriefs, one internally for all involved within the company, and the second with the contractors, PR consultants and ad agency. There may also need to be reconciliation meetings with your suppliers to agree their bills.

The ideal time for debriefs is 10–14 days after the event. Hold a meeting too soon and you will find that several people will have taken time off or be busy sorting out crises that arose while they were away. Leave it too long and people will have moved on, forgetting the passion they felt at the time. They also tend to adopt a 'political' bias on what went wrong and who did well. Departments close ranks and memories get synchronised to avoid blame.

The objectives of a debrief are to assess what can be improved for the next project, correcting what was below standard and building on what worked well.

■ Agendas

Always circulate an agenda before the debrief meeting and allow a fixed time for each topic. I like to run through events chronologically because that is the way I remember them. Meetings being meetings, big issues sail through without a problem, while everybody gets excited over some relatively unimportant detail.

■ The emotive bits

So a debrief is only worth something if it is completely honest, although I avoid emotive words like 'blame', 'useless' and 'rubbish', however strongly I feel. Nevertheless, if somebody responsible for doing a task fell short, it should be reported. Ending up with a fair and true report is often very difficult. You still need a contribution from those who failed to pull their weight. On the other hand, those who performed well will feel aggrieved if you fail to criticise those who didn't.

After the meeting, write a full report and circulate it.

■ Postal or telephone follow-up

Naturally you will follow up hot leads almost immediately. Then there is the huge bulk of mildly interested visitors. Once you have all these contacts transferred to your database, you can organise a mail shot to thank everybody for visiting.

It seems a shame just to ask if there is anything further you can help them with. If they were truly impressed with what they experienced, you need to push the contact forward by inviting them to a seminar, booking a factory visit or arranging a personal presentation on your latest range. Explain that time was limited at the show and there were many distractions. What you need is their undivided attention.

Better still, get the sales force to phone round. They will be able to generally chat about the exhibition, then can home in on the real objective, moving the relationship forward through a meeting.

When is the best time to do your follow-up? Probably a couple of weeks or so after the event. Both you and your prospect will have had urgent business to attend to on return and after a short gap they may be more amenable to your approach.

■ Visitor audits

In addition to adding names to your database, you should be able to build a visitor profile. You will have information on the industry sectors represented, the sizes of business, degree of interest and status of contacts. Apart from any internal marketing interest, this is very useful in evaluating the event and can give you considerable bargaining power when negotiating for next year.

■ Website report

Many companies have realised that they can put post-show news either on their existing website or set up a special one with limited access for the contacts they have made.

There is so much you can say, like:

- Reminder of products on display.
- Frequently-asked questions at the show and answers.
- Results of any competitions you ran.

- Quotable quotes from visitors.
- Names, pictures and telephone numbers of those who were on the stand for visitors who have lost your business cards.
- Details of your future exhibition activity if you don't mind your competitors knowing as well.
- Guest book for comments.

■ Press releases

Few companies forget the press release that goes out to tell the world how well they have done. Most are boring, giving the numbers of visitors and level of business, but if you have a human interest story resulting from the show, your release will soar above the others in the eyes of both newspaper editors and readers. Maybe you renewed relations with a company you hadn't dealt with for 20 years. Possibly a group of students has asked to do a project based on your products as a result of the welcome you gave them. It could be the response of the charity that you gave the carpet and stand furniture to. Ask around and seek out that interesting angle.

■ The next show

It's always relatively simple to get decisions on the next show while everybody is still basking in the warm glow of the last one. The 'high' won't last for ever. Once you allow the bickering to start, views become distorted.

Also, when the next show seems a long way off it is easier to agree timescales, budgets and responsibilities. Nobody is under threat and there isn't yet any competition from other distractions. First come, first served.

However, be realistic. Don't commit people to schedules and tasks that you know will prove difficult, even if they agree willingly for now. Being let down at the last minute is still being let down, whoever's fault it is.

What about the other scenario? The show did not meet expectations. You want to make sure the next one will. How do you motivate your superiors and colleagues to continue? You must be entirely honest. Admit the mistakes and put in place plans to overcome them next time. Then convince people that the show should be an integral part of your marketing policy. If you can demonstrate that it is still the most cost-effective way of attaining your targets, you are in with a chance.

A good way to present your case is to draft a chart of strengths and weaknesses. After everyone has had a chance to comment, examine each factor in turn. In the case of weaknesses, every person will have an input because improvement is clearly necessary. That is good.

In the case of strengths, you also want input on building on these. This is usually not so forthcoming, first because it requires imagination. Second, there is always a feeling that if something ain't broke, don't fix it. It also requires work which at face value does not appear to be necessary. Strengths lead to greater opportunities.

Let's look at an example. The demonstrations were very popular. Most played to full houses. That is good. So what are the opportunities that could arise from this:

- Would more space for the demonstration draw yet more spectators? If so, how would you handle them?
- Would shorter demos allow for more to be put into the programme, thus allowing an increase in spectator throughput without increasing handling problems?
- Are you doing enough to establish relationships with serious spectators? With the large numbers who arrive suddenly and drift away afterwards, it is difficult to pick out those with a genuine interest. Is there any way of making contact with them?
- Is there currently any means of assessing spectator reaction to the demo? What if a questionnaire were included in the publicity pack with an incentive to return it at or after the show?

And so you could go on. There is nothing so good that it can't be improved.

Chapter 19

Storage and Refurbishment

Now it's time to sit back and ponder about your longer term exhibiting plans.

The Argonaut will no doubt have been disturbed at some stage to learn that the wondrous structure that he's been bragging about to his cronies doesn't belong to him at all. It's rented. When you mentioned that this is a form of 'outsourcing', he is placated. He is still in his outsourcing phase and anything that is called outsourcing is OK with him.

If your exhibiting does eventually justify you owning your own stand, there are other considerations to be taken into account. The main one is the life of the stand. In the case of a custom-built affair, one or two years will be the maximum, the reasons being:

- The law of diminishing returns says that as a stand gets older, the costs in refurbishment to bring it back to show condition become increasingly unviable.
- Visitors get to recognise stands that they have seen before, particularly if they are of distinctive design, which is not good if you have a stated policy of innovation.
- Corporate culture and policies move on, so it is surprising how soon a stand will feel out of step with new initiatives.
- Stand staff achieve more when stimulated. It is difficult to work up more enthusiasm on a stand you have worked on possibly a dozen times.

If you have opted for a system approach, the inventory of components should give you reasonable flexibility. There will always be a certain 'sameness' of style, but you should be able to alter the floor plan and experiment with different panels and finishes.

■ Storage

Exhibition stands cannot just be dumped in a lock-up and forgotten until just before the next show. They need clean, dry, vermin-free space that is accessible to large vehicles. And it needs regular visits to check that everything is fine.

You have various choices:

- Ask your contractor to store it for you. The downside is that it will cost you, and occasionally bits get borrowed to sort out someone else's crisis. The upside is that the conditions should be (and I would check this is so) ideal and, when you come to use it next time, it is already in the right place.
- Use a storage area at your own premises. Make certain the space is up to standard and that the warehouse manager won't decide to ask you to leave at a moment's notice. If you have your own storeroom, keep it spotless. Your stand might not be the crown jewels but it is practically as priceless to you.
- Hire outside warehouse space or a small industrial unit. I have seen good and bad. One large company I worked for kept all its system components on the sixth floor of a warehouse in south London. Getting the bits in and out was a nightmare. Security was also a problem as everything was wrapped in hessian. Every time we went to inspect, someone had disturbed the covering to see what the curious shaped objects were, and because the inventory had been lost it wasn't possible to tell if anything had been taken. Perhaps worst of all was the dust. Felt-covered panels needed constant recovering. I'm sure not all warehouses are like this, but don't let them get away with poor service or lack of security.

■ Damp

Damp is the main problem in storage. A place that seems snug and dry in the summer will often develop condensation in the cold of winter.

Especially vulnerable is metalwork. Large trusses are mainly aluminium, which requires little maintenance because the metal oxidises on the surface forming an impervious barrier. Chromium-plated components, however, soon become pitted if kept in damp conditions. The best preventative measure is to wipe them over with a slightly oily rag and wrap them in old felt or other absorbent fabric.

Felt panel coverings also suffer badly from damp, which attacks the adhesive and areas become detached and discoloured. If this is a problem in your storage facilities, either accept that the panels will need periodic recladding or switch to a more durable surface.

■ Dust

Dust seems to settle in great quantities in most storage facilities I have used. Even when the place has been thoroughly cleaned out and sealed, it only takes a couple of months for a thin layer to settle again, so the obvious answer is dust sheets.

Complex components like trusses, which are often stacked separately, are the very devil to brush clean and are best pressure-washed.

■ Sunlight

The direct rays of the sun will fade graphics and fabric surfaces in a very short time. If you are taking on new storage facilities, check that there is not a skylight or large clear window. You might not be aware of the hazard on a dull day. Dust sheets are a simple solution.

■ Cases

If you have a stand that might experience any rough handling at all, have packing cases made. If you ship it abroad, they will certainly be necessary. The initial cost is more than justified. Have them made at the same time as the stand is constructed. It is easier for the contractor when they have the plans to hand and it normally eases any storage problems in the workshops as finished bits can be packed away neatly.

Cases are costly. But that has to be weighed against saving on refurbishment and damage. If you are a regular exhibitor, you probably come out about even, but the saving in stress is worth it.

There is, of course, one difficulty. Weight. Good strong cases mean that what would be a two-man lift becomes a fork-lift job. So you might need extra equipment on site.

■ Refurbishment

Stands used more than once must be expertly refurbished for each outing. Make certain you get a quote for this at the start of your exhibition season and if possible get it put into the contract. Refurbishment isn't just touching up with a dab of paint here and there. Done properly it means replacing any surface that has suffered the slightest damage. This is because it is usually impossible to get a perfect match. This is especially true of textured or clad surfaces. Blemishes often don't show in the workshop, but they will become obvious under the bright show lighting.

I recommend keeping a file with a panel-by-panel history and specification. This means that you don't have to sort through all your stock every time you want to use some of it.

■ Practical surfaces

Some surfaces are easier to refurbish than others. There is much to be said for a plain paint finish. Although it will probably need to be renewed for every show, the job is easy and quick to do. Felt is also very practical and will survive a bit of rough handling. Contractors are also quite good at 'invisible' repairs to felt covering, provided the patch comes from the same batch as the original.

Chapter 20

The Future of Exhibiting

'Blue sky thinking. That's the secret of my success.' Jason is in one of his philosophical moods and you just have to let him ramble on. 'Look to the future. Think outside the box.' Another article from an airline magazine.

Yet he is right. We must push forward the boundaries. Exhibitions are still an expanding medium, but they are competing in a gigantic media fairground for buyers' attention. Budgets are finite. New and fashionable media forms are clamouring for an increasing share of the publicity pound. You have to consider whether the money spent on your exhibition might not be better allocated to improving your website. In most cases, of course, it isn't an 'either/or' situation but the achievement of the right balance of cost-effectiveness.

■ The technological threat

Technological advances, like broadband communications, are an increasing threat to exhibitions. In the past, the best way to compare the offerings of different manufacturers and gather information was to attend the trade fair. Now everything is available at the click of a mouse in minutes. You can download videos, detailed plans and complex specifications. Your supplier can receive your Excel files or database, run a simulation and have the results back to you in a day. If you need to discuss anything, you can pop into your video conferencing suite and talk face to face with people from all over the world.

So why would visitors still want to attend an exhibition? Why not, as some have suggested, have a virtual stand sent to your PC, where you can wander round in 3D space and hear the pitch from virtual salesperson? You would have the whole stand to yourself, with no interruptions. Videos would start when you wanted to watch them.

All this would overcome the single biggest drawback with exhibitions as a medium – they are held so infrequently. Some major trade fairs are held only once every two years. In between, developments are being made and new products launched, and trade fairs rarely coincide with these. There is no doubt that exhibitions are perhaps the most inconvenient of media.

On the other hand, the virtual stand scenario ignores the most attractive features of an exhibition – the very experience of escaping from the office environment, and a commitment from both visitors and exhibitors to see and be seen. The mere fact that an exhibition is held annually makes it a special event, to be looked forward to, savoured and then remembered. In the same way that we crave live entertainment after watching months of television, we enjoy face-to-face contact with people who are normally only names attached to emails.

■ Organic growth

While I believe we can defend exhibitions against threat, there is no miraculous development around the corner that will knock competitive media for six. Growth has been steady and will continue to be so. Any changes will, in the main, be market-driven and the market in this instance is quite conservative.

■ The Future for Venues

If we assume that the exhibition experience is one of the main reasons why visitors attend (or not), then we must make the overall experience as pleasurable as possible.

The experience starts when the visitor leaves home. Frustration with accumulated travel, accommodation, parking and registration problems puts the visitor into a less than receptive mood when he or she eventually enters the hall. So the first line of responsibility rests with venues, hotels and airlines. They have recognised this and are trying, often against tremendous odds, to make the process of getting to your stand easier and less stressful.

■ Travel

For me, travelling is the biggest deterrent to attending exhibitions.

Air travel always seems a wasted opportunity. What should be a pleasant way to move about the globe is spoilt by petty officialdom, ridiculous fare structures and unnecessarily long waits in boring departure lounges. When you board the plane, the penny-pinching airlines squeeze your legs into an impossibly small space and make you breath stale air.

It may be too much to expect airports and airlines to change their attitude towards exhibition visitors, but I do wish there were more smiles, more attempts to understand us and more sincere apologies when things go wrong.

Trains in the UK are ridiculously expensive and, since privatisation, devoid of any logical system. So driving, except for the long haul, is the only option. However, when we get there, parking and security are a nightmare. Venues generally should devote more energy to sorting out parking arrangements, and if they are not adequate should arrange park-and-ride systems from off-site parks.

■ Large venues

Large venues especially are improving out of all recognition. New ones are opening, and the existing ones seeking to compete have invested huge sums to upgrade facilities and ambience. Considerable attention is being given to infrastructure, with stations and hotels being incorporated in the complexes. They really are trying to make things convenient.

On a global scale, venue expansion is taking place at a rate unmatched by the exhibitions industry. There is a shift away from the traditional western locations, with money being poured into facilities in the Middle and Far East. As the economies of China, Malaysia and India gather momentum, many of us will have to travel further afield to promote our goods. So we can expect worldwide competition to be fierce.

■ Smaller venues

Smaller venues in the UK don't seem to be matching this level of activity. There is a widening gap between the middle-sized venues and those at the bottom of the scale.

In many cases it is difficult for regional venues to improve structural and location problems. The old corn exchanges and market halls are beautiful structures that are rightly protected by preservation orders and cannot economically be adapted to the needs of today's exhibition organiser. Hotels, with several notable exceptions, also find it difficult to adapt.

Unfortunately many of the newly-built structures have been (and probable are still being) erected with basic flaws in the design of their function facilities. Ceilings are too low, lifts too small and access difficult for anything larger than a Transit van. This is probably fine for the average wedding reception, but is totally inadequate if they want to attract the smaller trade fair or roadshow. Often they are over-specified, and exhibition organisers resent having to pay for facilities they don't really need.

I suggest that what we need are versions of the large venues scaled down to serve small exhibitions, roadshows and regional affairs. We require little more than large industrial units, with easy access and gigantic car parks. They don't need to be in town centres; in fact, since most visitors come by car and stay less than a day, they are better placed on greenfield sites near major road junctions. I have in mind something like structures used by large car auctions.

■ The package trip

Most of the exhibitions I get involved in are in major venues. And every time, I have to make all the arrangements to attend myself. I would really welcome a service similar to that from a holiday travel agent – when I book my ticket for the show, the organisers could arrange my travel, accommodation, hire car, travel insurance and offer a special deal if I decide to stay over for a few days. In my view, this level of service could be made standard. I haven't yet come across any venue that has worked out a practical and attractive package deal.

■ Coping in a dangerous world

We are all conscious of the dangers of worldwide travel. Most of us take the view that the odds of anything happening to us are remote. The statistics are on our side. How many exhibition visitors have been harmed by terrorist outrages?

However, if the level of terrorism goes up, we may all start to question the wisdom of international trips to big cities. In the UK, roughly a third[1] of exhibitions take place in London. London is a focus for terrorist activity and places where people congregate will be especially at risk. In conditions like this we may think twice before undertaking trips to international trade fairs, especially in high-risk localities.

How can the exhibition industry respond? The initial approach is to step up security, although this does little to help. The measures are an added nuisance and are next to useless against a determined suicide bomber.

The obvious approach is to split the big international events into national affairs and hold these at provincial locations within each

---

1 *UK Exhibition Facts*, published by the Exhibition Venues Association, 15 Keeble Court, Fairmeadows, North Seaton, Northumberland NE63 9SF, tel. +44 (0)1670 818801. Price £200 plus VAT.

country. It will be sad to miss the great shindigs in Vegas, Hamburg and London, but preferable to giving up altogether.

■ The Industry Structure

Trends within the industry suggest a slow but relentless move towards consolidation among the larger organisers, which will end with a handful of powerful groups. This may reduce your bargaining power, but it should also mean a higher level of service. Having said that, there always seem to be entrepreneurs who are willing to risk entering at the bottom end to fill a niche need. Perhaps we can see a polarisation in the future into a few large groups and many small specialist organisers.

Trends also indicate that business-to-business exhibitions are fragmenting into smaller and more focused events. Combined with the advances in database management, this should result in more accurate targeting of visitors.

Many of the large traditional consumer shows plod on year after year, while new ones are being launched off the back of TV shows and media circuses. These shows tend to indicate a greater integration across the media. In recent years, the BBC's Clothes Show was a good example. I think we will see many more in the future.

■ The Future Stand

The future holds exciting possibilities for stand-holders. What we must remember is that the basic requirements don't change. There has to be space for salespeople to sell, there have to be displays and there have to be presentations.

I have heard it forecast that stands will tend to be smaller, but as I have already stated, a stand has to be of the right size to attain its objectives. I see no advances in design or technology that can change that.

■ Interactive displays

What can be improved is the interactivity of displays. Museums are learning this lesson. Children no longer want to read about exhibits. They want to handle and manipulate them. They want to learn through physical experiment. Interactivity is a key to communication in the future, and exhibitions provide exactly the right environment.

■ Harnessing new technology

With all this exciting new technology, surely there is much we can use to promote ourselves and our products. Indeed there is. But we must use what enhances our offering, not just technology for technology's sake:

- Large screen and projection technology combined with high definition television will mean unprecedented visual imagery.
- Broadband communications will allow live links to other sites, such as an international corporate newsroom, construction sites showing daily progress or a sponsored entry in a yacht race.
- Computer games. Armed forces recruiting teams have always recognised the value of sim games on stands. Now games technology is becoming more and more useful for corporate marketing.

■ New materials and styles

New, exciting materials are becoming available all the time. We would love to use them, but it is often difficult to get fire certificates and clearance to build them into stands.

There is, I believe, a tendency towards a more minimalist approach. If we increase the use of free-standing interactive elements, we don't need so many solid walls. This aids in shipping and storage. Taken to the extreme, we could use a simple frame and fabric structure. Then everything can be packed away into a surprisingly small space.

■ A Fitting End

It arrives, not by email as usual, but by typed memo. 'Jason Barber-Browne will shortly be leaving his post as Chief Executive of International Spigots to take up a new appointment as Managing Director of Superbronze Tanning Studios. You are invited to his leaving party on Friday in the reception room at The Crown at 6.00pm.' A bolt from the blue.

At the party, Jason corners you. 'We done OK on the exhibition front, didn't we? I met Princess Anne, we were on the telly three times, and made Allied Grubscrews look pretty stupid when we nobbled the drinks at their launch. Good fun, eh?'

'Yeah, Jason. Good fun.'

The man is impossible. That you had a stand that everybody in the company was proud of, worked up a team that performed like Man U and, best of all, exceeded all the targets seems to matter little to the Argonaut. Fun was what really mattered to him. Then again, would we really go through all that pain if there weren't an element of fun?

'Tell you what, why not come and be my new marketing director? I could arrange a better package than you're getting now. You'd love Superbronze. Our sort of company, know what I mean?'

'No thanks, Jason, there are one or two things I'd like to finish here before moving on.' You wouldn't tell him the true reason, would you?

Nevertheless, you had to agree on one point. Yes, we done OK.

Appendix

■ Useful Websites

■ Trade bodies

www.abco.org.uk
Association of British Professional Conference Organisers

www.aeo.org.uk
Association of Exhibition Organisers

www.bacd.org.uk
British Association of Conference Destinations

www.beca.org.uk
British Exhibition Contractors Association

www.visitbritain.com
British Tourist Authority

www.britishtourismpartnership.com
British Tourism Partnership

www.ukti.gov.uk
Department of Trade and Industry

www.exhibitionvenues.com
Exhibition Venues Association

■ International bodies

www.aipc.org
Association Internationale des Palais des Congres

www.efct.com
European Federation Conference Tours

www.iacvb.org
International Association of Convention and Business Bureaus

www.iccaworld.com
The International Congress and Conference Association

■ Publications

www.citmagazine.com
Conference and Incentive Travel

www.mashmedia.com
Exhibition Bulletin
Exhibition News

www.eventmagazine.co.uk
Event Magazine

www.meetpie.com
Meetings and Incentive Travel

■ Directories

www.eventservicesonline.co.uk
Corporate Event Services

Index